Pelican Books
How Children Learn

John Holt was born in New York City on 14 April 1923. He
was educated at a number of schools in the States and
at Le Rosey in Switzerland (1935–6), after which he attended
the Phillips Exeter Academy and graduated in 1939. He
took a B.S. degree in Industrial Administration at Yale
from 1940 to 1943. Following this he served in the Submarine
service of the U.S. Navy until 1946. He then worked in
various parts of the world government movement, finally
as Executive Director of the New York State branch of the
United Work Federalists. On returning to the States in
1953 after travelling in Europe for a year he taught in
various schools in Colorado and Massachusetts. He is
presently advising consultant at the Fayerweather Street
School in Cambridge, Massachusetts. His publications
include *How Children Fail* and *How Children Learn*, both
available in Penguins. He has also published articles and
reviews in such magazines and journals as the *New York
Review of Books*, *Book Week* and *Peace News* (London)

John Holt

How Children Learn

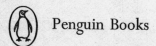 Penguin Books

Penguin Books Ltd, Harmondsworth,
Middlesex, England
Penguin Books Australia Ltd, Ringwood,
Victoria, Australia

First published in the U.S.A. by Pitman Publishing
Corporation 1967
Published in Pelican Books 1970
Reprinted 1971

Made and printed in Great Britain by
Cox & Wyman Ltd,
London, Reading and Fakenham
Set in Linotype Pilgrim

Contents

Foreword

How Children Fail described children using their minds badly. This book tries to describe children – in a few cases, adults – using their minds well, learning boldly and effectively. Some of the children described are in school; most are not yet old enough. It is before they get to school that children are likely to do their best learning. Many experts agree that this is so, though they differ about the reason. I believe, and try to show here, that in most situations our minds work best when we use them in a certain way, and that young children tend to learn better than grown-ups (and better than they themselves will when they are older) because they use their minds in a special way. In short, children have a style of learning that fits their condition, and which they use naturally and well until we train them out of it. We like to say that we send children to school to teach them to think. What we do, all too often, is to teach them to think badly, to give up a natural and powerful way of thinking in favour of a method that does not work well for them and that we rarely use ourselves.

What are the results? Only a few children in school ever become good at learning in the way we try to make them learn. Most of them get humiliated, frightened, and discouraged. They use their minds, not to learn, but to get out of doing the things we tell them to do – to make them learn. In the short run, these strategies seem to work. They make it possible for many children to get through their schooling even though they learn very little. But in the long run these strategies are self-limiting and self-defeating, and destroy both character and intelligence. The children who use such strategies are prevented by them from growing into more than limited versions of the human beings they might have become. This is the real failure that takes place in school; hardly any children escape.

When we better understand the ways, conditions, and spirit in which children do their best learning, and are able to make school into a place where they can use and improve the style of thinking and learning natural to them, we may be able to prevent much of this failure. School may then become a place in which *all* children grow, not just in size, not even in knowledge, but in curiosity, courage, confidence, independence, resourcefulness, resilience, patience, competence, and understanding. To find how best to do this will take us a long time. We may find, in fifty or a hundred years, that all of what we think of as our most up-to-date notions about schools, teaching, and learning, are either completely inadequate or outright mistaken. But we will make a big step forward if, by understanding children better, we can undo some of the harm we are now doing.

This book is more concerned to describe effective learning than to explain it, or give a theory about it. In many places men are busy trying to find out what goes on in the brain, electrically, chemically, and otherwise, when we think and learn. Such research is interesting and may prove to be useful, but it has nothing to do with the aims of this book. We do not need to learn more about the brain, as an organ, in order to make schools better. We could make them a great deal better, knowing no more about the brain than most people know right now. Thus it is interesting that men should be finding evidence that experiences are stored in the brain, in the shape of complicated molecules, like file cards stored in a file. What teachers and learners need to know is what we have known for some time: first, that vivid, vital, pleasurable experiences are the easiest to remember, and secondly, that memory works best when unforced, that it is not a mule that can be made to walk by beating it. It is interesting to read Wolfgang Köhler's theory, perhaps now held by many others, that electrical fields are set up in the brain when we perceive, think and feel.

This would certainly account for the fact that we think badly, and even perceive badly, or not at all, when we are anxious and afraid. But we don't need the explanation to know that the fact is a fact, and to learn from it that when we make children afraid we stop their learning dead in its tracks.

This book is more about children than about child psychology. I hope those who read it will come to feel, or feel more than when they opened it, that children are interesting and worth looking at. I hope that when they look they will notice many things they never noticed before, and in these find much food for thought. I want to whet their curiosity and sharpen their vision, even more than to add to their understanding; to make them sceptical of old dogmas, rather than give them new ones.

The human mind, after all, is a mystery, and, in large part, will probably always be so. It takes even the most thoughtful, honest, and introspective person many years to learn even a small part of what goes on in his own mind. How, then, can we be sure about what goes on in the mind of another? Yet many people talk as if we could measure and list the contents of another person's mind as easily, accurately, and fully as the contents of a suitcase. This is not to say that we ought not to try to understand more about other people's minds, and thoughts, but only that we must be very modest and tentative about what we think we have found out.

There's an old story about two men on a train. One of them seeing some naked-looking sheep in a field, said, 'Those sheep have just been sheared.' The other looked a moment longer, and then said, 'They seem to be – on this side.' It is in such a cautious spirit that we should say whatever we have to say about the workings of the mind, and it is in this spirit that I have tried to write, and in which I hope others will read, this book.

Games and Experiments

9 August 1960

I am sitting on a friend's terrace. Close by is Lisa, 16 months old, a bright and bold child. She has invented a very varied pseudo-speech which she uses all the time. Some sounds she says over and over again, as if she meant something by them. She likes to touch and handle things, and is surprisingly dexterous; she can fit screws and similar small objects into the holes meant for them. Can it be that little children are less clumsy than we have always supposed?

One of Lisa's favourite games is to take my ball-point pen out of my pocket, take the top off, and then put it on again. This takes some skill. She never tires of the game; if she sees me with the pen in my pocket, she lets me know right away that she wants it. There is no putting her off. She is stubborn, and if I pretend – which is a lie – not to know what she wants, she makes a scene. The trick, when I know I will need to use my pen, is to have an extra one hidden in a pocket.

The other day she was playing on the piano, hitting out more or less at random with both hands, pleased to be working the machine, and making such an interesting noise. Curious to see whether she would imitate me, I bounced up and down the keyboard with my index finger. She watched, then did the same.

11 August 1960

Yesterday I had the portable electric typewriter on the terrace. The older children were looking at it and using it. Lisa was busy eating an ice-cream cone and, for a while at least, was not interested. When the cone was gone, however, she came to see what the others were doing, and soon asked, by sounds and signs, to be picked up and given a chance. So I sat her on my lap in front of the machine. Having seen me poke at the keys, one finger at a time, she did the same, and seemed pleased by what happened – something flew through the air and made a sharp click, and there was a general impression of activity and motion, and mysterious things going on inside the machine, things that she was making happen.

Now and then she would hit more than one key at a time, and keys would get stuck. I would then turn off the machine and straighten them out. After seeing me turn the rotary On-Off switch a few times, she tried to turn it herself, but her fingers weren't strong enough. When this happened, she reached down, took my right hand, brought it up to the switch, and made me work it. Soon we had a good game going. I would turn off the typewriter; she would try for a while to turn it back on; then she would take my hand and make me do it.

She also liked the carriage-return lever. Each time I returned the carriage for a new line, she would take hold of the lever and give it one more push. Only rarely did she get excited and begin to slam and bang on the keys. Once she showed me that she wanted me to put the typewriter on the ground I did so, but soon saw that this was a mistake; she wanted to climb on and even into it, to see what was really going on inside. After a bit of an argument and tussle I got it back up on the table. We were busy with all this for about forty minutes. Perhaps the attention span of infants is not as short as we think.

Today, with her elder brother more or less in charge, Lisa was in more of a banging mood, and often slapped the keyboard with her hands. Each time she did this, we turned the machine off and carefully unscrambled the stuck keys. Since this slowed up the action, I thought it might in time show her that it was not a good idea to slap the keyboard. But it was also interesting for her to watch us unstick the keys. After this had happened a number of times, I suggested to her brother that next time she piled the keys up we turn off the machine and just wait to see what she would do. We did so. She poked a key or two, but nothing happened. Then, seeming to notice that the machine was not making its usual busy hum, she reached up herself and pulled back the stuck keys.

24 July 1961

This morning Lisa bent down to pick up a balloon and, as she did, a puff of wind coming through the door blew the balloon across the floor. She watched it go. When it stopped, she moved close to it, and blew at it, as if to make it go farther. This surprised me. Can such young children make a connexion between the ability of the wind to move objects, and their own ability to move them by blowing on them? Apparently they can.

One game almost all babies seem to like is to have you blow across their hands or fingers, moving your head from side to side so that the airstream moves back and forth. They smile; then after a while they begin to investigate where this mysterious stuff is coming from, and try to poke a finger into your mouth. They find it interesting that you can get a similar effect by fanning them with a fan, or piece of cardboard.

Later, Lisa walked round and round the balloon, singing, more or less, her own version of 'Ring-around-a-rosie'. As she sang it, she began to change it, until before long it had become an entirely different song. Much of what she says, sings, and does, is like this; it starts out as one thing, and gradually turns into another. A musician might call it variations on a theme.

Many other little children I have known love to tell endless stories and sing endless songs. Sometimes the song is about what they did or would like to do. A mother told me that her four-year-old boy, whose seven-year-old sister was in school, began one day, alone in his room, to chant a song about, 'I wish I had a sister, who didn't have to go to school, and would do everything I say. . . .' Often the song is nonsensical, words and nonsense syllables; sometimes sense and nonsense are mixed. Many children like to play a game with a grown-up, in which each takes turns adding something to the song. It is not as easy as it sounds. Trying to make up words and music at the same time is a strain on the imagination, and what comes out is usually no better than what the child does, and, as a rule, very much like it.

These are good games, and we might do well to encourage them, pay attention to them, take part in them, both at home and in school.

Children first going to school do a lot of singing, to be sure; but they all sing the same songs, taught and led by the teacher, and the aim is to get them 'right', not to make up something new. Some children like this and get good at it; for others, it just becomes one more of those things that you have to do in school – compulsory fun, as so much of early school is. Many of these children become non-singers, a needless waste. The work of Carl Orff and others who have used his method of instruction suggests that when children are given many opportunities to improvise, to make up their own chants, rhythms, and tunes, their musical and verbal growth can be very rapid.

25 July 1961

Cries from the living room announce a new collision between Lisa and the institution of private property. She is interested in everything she sees, wants to examine it, handle it, test it, take it apart if she can. Naturally, she has no sense of what is valuable, or fragile, or dangerous. Having seen me plug in the electric typewriter, she was eager to plug it in herself, and fiercely resented being told that she was not to fool around with electric sockets. The other day she managed to turn on all the burners on top of the stove, fortunately far enough so that the pilot light was able to light them. She did not like being told to leave the stove alone. It's impossible for her to see why she should not be allowed to touch what everyone else touches. When she takes things, she never thinks to put them back where she got them – even if she could remember where she got them.

There is no very good or easy answer to this problem. Every day we find ourselves saying, 'No, no, don't touch that, it's too hot, it's too sharp, it will hurt you, it will break, it belongs to me, I need it.' Each time she feels, naturally, that we are attacking her right and need to investigate every part of the world around her so that she may make some sense out of it. Everyone else touches this; why can't I? It is easy to see how too much of such treatment could destroy a child's curiosity, and make him feel that the world, instead of being full of interesting things to explore and think about, is full of hidden dangers and ways of getting into trouble.

We try to solve the problem by giving Lisa toys of her own, and telling her to leave other things alone. This doesn't work very well. For one thing, the toys aren't interesting enough. For another, she can't remember, even if she wants to, what she is free to touch, and what not. Most important, it is the fact that older and bigger people use various objects around the house that makes these objects so interesting. Like all little children, Lisa wants to be like the big people, and do what they do. When dishes are being washed, she demands to be allowed to help; when cooking is going on, she wants to cook; when lemonade is being made, she wants to help make it. And she will not be put off by obviously phony substitutes.

It is hard not to feel that there must be something very wrong with much of what we do in school, if we feel the need to worry so much about what many people call 'motivation'. A child has no stronger desire than to make sense of the world, to move freely in it, to do the things that he sees bigger people doing. Why can't we make more use of this great drive for understanding and competence? Surely we can find more ways to let children see people using some of the skills we want them to acquire – though this will be difficult when in fact those skills, like many of the 'essential' skills of arithmetic, are not really *used* to do anything. Who, in real life, divides one fraction by another?

Meanwhile, at home, we should try to keep out of reach, and even out of sight, valuable or dangerous objects that we don't want children to touch. At the same time, we should keep on hand a good many objects cheap and durable enough so that a child can touch them and use them; we shouldn't have to worry if they get broken. Maybe certain ordinary household objects would be good presents for small children: an eggbeater, a saucepan, a flashlight. After all, it doesn't make much sense, in a family that will later spend tens of thousands of dollars on the child's education, to get upset, and to upset him, because he may ruin something worth twenty-five cents. I have so often seen people in drugstores or supermarkets, where there is very little that a child could spoil or break, and where anything he did break would hardly cost over a dollar, get all upset because he is touching, feeling, picking up the various things he sees. Why not? This is how he learns about them. If he moves something out of its proper place, it's easy enough to put it back.

It is probably a mistake, anyway, to assume that whatever little children touch, they will destroy, and that we must therefore keep them from touching anything that is not theirs. This dampens their curiosity and confidence. More than that, it probably makes them too fiercely possessive of what is their own. We should try instead, I think, to teach that respecting property does not mean never touching what is not yours, but means treating objects carefully, using them as they are meant to be used, and putting them back where they belong. Children are perfectly able to learn these things; they are less clumsy and destructive than we suppose. And it is only by handling and using objects that children can learn the right way to handle them. One of Maria Montessori's many valuable contributions to education was that she showed that very little children could easily be taught to move, not just exuberantly, but also deftly, precisely, gently.

30 July 1961

Little children love games, and can make them out of anything. This morning Lisa was in bed with her older sister, Nell.
First Nell would turn out the light over the bed, then Lisa would
turn it back on, saying, 'Don't turn it off.' The older girl would
move her hand slowly, slowly towards the light. Every time the
hand moved, Lisa would say, 'Don't turn it off.' This could be
dragged out a long time. Finally, off would go the light. Lisa
would then turn it on and the game would start again.

A lot of the games little children play begin as if by accident.
One day I took a magazine across the room, put it on a table,
and went to do something else. Lisa went to the table, took the
magazine off, put it on the floor, and then looked meaningfully
at me. I went back and put it on the table. She took it off. Soon
we had a fine game going, which lasted for some time.

The spirit behind such games should be a spirit of joy, foolish-
ness, exuberance, like the spirit behind all good games, including the game of trying to find out how the world works, which
we call education. But even in a more narrow sense games like
these are educational. They give a child a stronger feeling of
cause and effect, of one thing leading to another. Also, they help
a child to feel that he makes a difference, that he can have some
effect on the world around him. How exciting it must be for a
child, playing a game with an adult, to feel that by doing a certain thing, he can make that omnipotent giant do something,
and that he can keep this up as long as he likes.

Once, visiting friends in Chicago, I was left for a while one
morning in charge of the children – Alice, three-and-a-half,
and Patrick, just over two. They were used to playing on the
sidewalk of the rather quiet street where they live, so I told
them they could do this as long as they stayed in sight. But
they soon strayed out of sight, and I had to fetch them back,
protesting and wailing. They were furious. They told me that
I was bad, and that they were going to tell their mommy on

me. I told them to go ahead. Patrick then said that his mommy would spank me – 'Like this'. I pretended to cry. This is an absolutely foolproof game to play with little children; they all love it. Soon we had a game going. The little children would 'spank' me – slap me on the back – and I would pretend to cry. When I stopped, Patrick would say, 'I'm still spanking you,' and I would have to start again. Now and then I would say, 'I'm a good boy.' He would say, very firmly, 'You bad boy.' And so we went on for some time, until they found something else to do. Later we showed the game to the children's parents.

1 August 1961

Recently Lisa has started to play fierce games. She bares her teeth, growls, roars, rushes at me. I pretend to be afraid, and cower behind a chair. It can go on for some time. From this, and many other things she does, it seems as if she feels a *Me* inside her, growing stronger, doing things, demanding things. Any game that makes that *Me* seem more powerful must be a good game. Most of the time she knows all too well how powerless that *Me* is.

Sometimes she takes a stick and hits the seat of a chair with it, making the sound of an explosion with her mouth. As she hits the chair she blinks, as if the great force of her own blow scared her a little. It reminds me of a nine-year-old boy I knew who, when he first began to play soccer, and I think without knowing that he did it, made this same kind of explosive noise with his mouth every time he kicked the ball. It may be worth noting that he was not very big or athletic, and could not kick the ball very hard; had he been able to, he would not have needed the explosion-noise.

For all her fierceness, pride, and stubborn independence, Lisa is at heart kind and obliging. One game she likes to play is the 'you-can't' game. Sometimes it begins with me outside the screen door, she inside. She says, 'Can't come in.' I begin to pull gently on the door. She pulls as hard as she can from the other side. After a while, as if exhausted, I let go, and the door shuts with a small bang. She gives me a triumphant look, and again says, 'You can't come in.' Again I try the door, again she resists, until I let the door shut again. This may happen five or six times. But always, at the end, she lets me in, saying very sweetly, 'Come in, John.'

The other morning, hearing her talking to her sister, I went into their room. She gave me a flirty look and said, 'Go way.' 'Why?' I asked. She said, 'Because.' 'Because what?' She said, 'You have to.' 'But I don't want to.' She said, 'You need to,' this being even more emphatic than having to. I said again that I didn't want to. Then an odd thing happened. She said, 'You can't.' She had slipped into a pattern of answers that she ordinarily uses in different circumstances. At about this time I left the room. A moment later I came back, and the game began again. This time, after we had played a few times, she said, 'Don't go way.' Children don't mind letting us adults win the game, as long as we let them score a few points. But so many of us, like some football coaches, seem never to be content with merely winning; we have to run up the big score.

2 August 1961

The other day we went to Carlsbad Caverns, a strange and beautiful place. To get there, we rode many hours in the car. On the way, we played games. The radio was on and, with Lisa watching, I began to clap my hands in time to the music. She did the same. Then I began to clap one palm against the other fist. She watched a while, then made both her hands into fists, clapped together a bit, looked again, saw this wasn't right, and soon did what I was doing. From this grew a whole series of games. I clapped hand against head; so did she. I clapped hand against stomach; so did she. I made the games more complicated. I clapped head with one hand and stomach with another; or clapped head with one hand while holding that elbow with the other, and so on. It was most interesting to see how she copied what I was doing. Each time she began by doing something fairly quickly. As she did it, she checked what she was doing against what I was doing. Then she made a change in what she was doing, checked again, and so went on until she was satisfied that what we were both doing was the same. Watching her do this, I was struck by two things. First, she did not feel that she had to get everything right before she started to do anything. She was willing – no, more than willing, eager – to begin by doing *something*, and then think about fixing it up. Secondly, she was not satisfied with incorrect imitations, but kept on looking and comparing until she was satisfied that she was correct – which she almost always was.

An older child, playing this game, might well play it differently, and in doing so, get his imitation right the first time. He could do his imitating in his mind, checking to see whether he had it right before doing it with his body. Or, he could put my action into words, and then suit his action to the words. But very small children, at least this one, do not seem to work that way, can't carry out an act in their imagination and correct it there. They have to imitate, compare, and correct, all at the concrete or physical level, and continue until they get it right.

In one way – one of many, in fact – Lisa is strikingly different from the unsuccessful ten-year-olds I have known in school. She wants to get things right, and will stick at them until she does; they just want to get things over with and out of the way. Very young children seem to have what could be called an Instinct of Workmanship. We tend not to see it, because they are unskilful and their materials crude. But watch the loving care with which a little child smooths off a sand cake, or pats and shapes a mud pie. They want to make it as well as they can, not to please someone else, but to satisfy themselves.

3 August 1961

Watching Lisa, I am reminded often of Bill Hull's story about the first-grader who burst into tears upon hearing that the word 'once' was spelled O-N-C-E. What puzzles me is why six-year-olds should be so much more bothered by this kind of confusion and paradox than this baby. She hears things all day long that make no sense, but she doesn't appear to mind. She lives and moves in uncertainty as naturally and easily as a fish moves in water. When, and why, do children begin to crave certainty?

Children don't seem to be born fearful. Oh, there are a few things they seem to fear instinctively – loud noises and loss of support – though there are many babies who love to be tossed into the air and caught, or otherwise tumbled about. It looks very much as if children catch most of their fears from their elders.

Lisa, for example, never used to be afraid of bugs. When she saw any kind of crawling or flying thing, she wanted to pick it up and look at it. One day a twelve-year-old friend of her older sister came to visit. Lisa was in the room with the two older girls, when the visitor saw a spider in a corner. She began to scream hysterically, and kept on until they got her out of the room and killed the spider. Since then, Lisa has been afraid of all bugs – flies, moths, worms, anything. She has learned her lesson. She doesn't scream or carry on, only draws away from them and doesn't want to have anything to do with them. A part of her curiosity about the world and her trust in it has been shut off. Who can tell when it will turn on again?

Most of the fear that children catch is of a more subtle kind. They catch it bit by bit, in very small doses. The other day Lisa was playing with the electric portable typewriter. She can turn it on and off, and can work the carriage return. While typing away, she suddenly got the urge to bring both hands down on the keys. A bunch of keys flew up and stuck. She leaned over the keyboard to pull them back. I feared that as she tried to get the keys back she might touch a key on the keyboard, which would make another key come up and give her fingers a sharp rap. Also, I feared that in tugging back the keys she might bend some of them out of line. So I showed her again how to turn the machine off, and then carefully untangled the stuck keys.

Then she did an interesting bit of exploration. On each side of the keyboard there is a shift key, and on the left side a shift lock. She saw that when you push the shift key down, it comes back up, but when you push the shift lock down, it stays down, and the shift key with it. Then the problem is how to get them back up. Tugging does no good. After a while she found that if she pushed the shift key down it unlocked the shift lock, and both keys came up. Then she looked for a key on the right side that would do the same thing. The margin release did nothing that she could observe, and the tabulator key, much to her surprise, made the whole carriage slide over, and rang the bell into the bargain. After some more experimenting, she soon had the whole shift key and lock system figured out.

All this time I was standing to one side, about ten feet away. I wanted to see what she was doing; also I wanted to be able to shut the machine off if she should bang on all the keys again, or do anything else that might hurt her or the machine. I felt that I was watchful rather than anxious, but she must have sensed some quality of anxiety in my watchfulness, for as she worked with the machine she kept doing something she had never done when she was younger – looking up at me with an expression on her face that clearly seemed to ask, 'Is this all right?'

Children, particularly little ones, are very sensitive to emotion. They not only catch everything we feel, they blow it up to larger-than-life-size. Lisa begins to cry if any of her older brothers or sisters seem to be having a serious argument or fight. Even when they roughhouse in fun, she tries to pull them apart, pleading, 'Stop! Stop!' Often, in other families, I have

seen children unhappy for a long time because of an argument
between their parents, which the parents had done their best
to conceal. It need not even be parents. Once I was visiting
some friends, whose children I knew very well and was very
fond of. The mother and I got into an argument about politics.
While the argument was warm, it was not unfriendly; we are
generally on the same side of the fence. But even as much
warmth as there was in the argument was too much for the
children. They began to circle around and move in, in a concilia-
tory fashion, as if by giving us something else to think about
they might take our minds off the quarrel, and get everything
cheerful and happy again.

It is simply not true, or at least not always true, that little
children have no empathy, cannot feel what others feel. They
are, no doubt, often cruel to each other; but if they are near
another child who is badly hurt or very unhappy, they soon
become very distressed. It is a very rare child who is capable of
the kind of sustained, deliberate cruelty so often shown by
adults.

Often their cruelty may be experimental. Once I saw two
two-year-old boys playing side by side on the floor. They were
pushing cars and trucks around, and having a pleasant time. At
one point one of them picked up the fairly heavy metal truck
he was playing with, and looked at the other with a speculative
expression. I had a faint hunch that something bad was about
to happen, but I didn't feel I could say anything, because the
child's father, my host, whom I did not know well, was watching with me, and said nothing. But sure enough, in a moment
or so the little boy with the truck, looking very calm, picked
it up and smacked the other boy in the head with it. The other
little boy looked up amazed, and then burst into roars of pain
and dismay. The first little boy looked at him, puzzled, and
increasingly distressed (though his father for some reason
made no move to punish or reprove him). All these roars and
tears seemed to be more results than he had bargained for. He
did not cry himself, but he was clearly frightened and unhappy.

One of my earliest recollections – actually by now I remem-

ber the telling of it rather than the event itself – was of playing in the park with a friend my own age – about three,
perhaps four – who out of a clear blue sky hit me in the head
with his toy shovel. We had been playing peacefully; I never
understood, then or later, why he hit me. Perhaps it was this
same overpowering urge to see what would happen.

4 August 1961

Lisa remembers and likes to use phrases that carry some emo-
tional weight. Within the past few weeks I have heard her say,
for the first time, 'No fair', 'I'm making a mess!' 'Don't make
me mad!' and 'Quit it!' All of these are said at times of stress
and excitement. When she finds herself in such situations, such
phrases come naturally.

Her talk and games are connected. The other day, as we were
riding to town in the car, she in back, I in front, I turned around
to look at her. She looked mischievously at me, then said,
firmly, 'Turn around.' I had never heard her say it before. I
turned around. A moment later, I looked back at her again. She
said, 'Turn around,' and the game began. It went on for some
time.

Sometimes the game is reversed. The other morning she told
me to watch her, and began to walk round and round one of
the living-room chairs, her eye on me. I guessed that she wanted
me to say something about what she was doing, so I did.
Either the guess was right, or she was just as pleased with it
as with whatever she might have wanted. She went on doing,
first this, then that, all the while watching me and listening to
what I was saying. Indeed, quite often it seems that, just as
she says things to see what people will do, she does things to
hear what people will say.

6 August 1961

Not long ago Lisa was patting my cheek, I forget why. I puffed the cheek full of air, and waited. It was a tempting target. She gave it a light slap, and I let the air burst forth from between my lips with a very satisfactory noise. She was delighted, and asked me to do it again. Soon the whole family was playing this game with her. After a while, she invited us to play the game in reverse. She puffed out her already chubby cheek, but when we patted it there wasn't enough air pent up to make any sound. But this didn't seem to bother her; she enjoyed the game anyway.

For some time she has enjoyed games in which she imitated her elders. Now she is beginning to invent games in which we are supposed to imitate her. Like so many good games, this one began by accident. She was making a face, which she likes to do, when she caught my eye. With nothing in mind, I imitated the face. She made a different face. I imitated that one. Right away she saw that I was going to try to do whatever she did, and away we went.

Another time, her older brothers were playing, on the living-room floor, a game called leg-wrestling. After watching this a while, she insisted on being allowed to play. We did some mock leg-wrestles with her, sometimes pulling her over, sometimes making it look as if she had pulled us over – accompanied by many grunts and groans. Soon she began doing various stunts, which she asked us to copy, flopping down on her knees, turning round and round on hands and knees, looking backwards between her legs (a favourite with all little children), and so on. One morning she led me on a little walk through the pine woods that surround the house. Sometimes she ran, sometimes she walked, sometimes she kicked one foot in the air as she walked. All the while she watched me to see if I was imitating, and imitating properly.

9 August 1961

The other day we went to a small amusement park in town. It has a tiny ferris wheel, a train that goes round an oval track, a jeep that goes with locked wheels in a fixed circle around a post, and a ring of little metal cars that bump noisily around a circular wooden track.

From the first day, Lisa was fascinated by the cars. We put her in one, and off she went. We thought the noise and bumps might frighten her, and clearly she was on the verge of being frightened. As she went round and round, she had a set expression on her face, and only occasionally looked at us as she went by. Going round, counterclockwise, she kept turning the little steering wheel of her car. It seemed that she was always turning it to the left. Was this just a coincidence? Or had she grasped something, riding in the real car, about the relationship between the turning of the wheel and the movement of the car?

Soon the ride ended and we looked for something else to do. Some bigger children were riding around in the little train, blowing the whistle and ringing the bell. To Lisa, it looked interesting and just a bit frightening. Perhaps the train made too much noise, perhaps it was too big, too black. She kept saying, 'I can't go train, I can't go train.' We said that was all right, she didn't have to. The cars remained her favourites.

After a while, we left the park to go get some ice cream. As we ate it, her mental picture of the train began to be less terrifying. The more she thought about it, the smaller and safer it looked. She began to say, very boldly, 'I need to ride that train *right now*!' We felt she should have this chance to conquer her fear, so back we went. But, alas, when we got there the train looked just as big and black as ever, and she said, 'I can't go train, I can't go train.'

It is easy to say, much of the time, why we fear the things we do. It is not easy to say from where the drive to overcome these fears comes, particularly in a very little child. Some kinds of courage are learned, but there is surely also an instinct of courage, a wish to be brave, to overcome fear. It will grow if we do not put more strain on it than it can bear. We should give it every encouragement.

When Lisa wants to do something very much, she says, 'I have to.' When she does not want to do something, she says, 'I can't.' It is easy to see where these expressions came from. When we want her to do something, we say, 'You have to.' When we want her not to do something, we say, 'You can't.' She just turns the words back on us. She is just beginning to be aware of the conflict of will between her and the giants who run everything. Her big brother, a grown-up to her, often plays a game with her. He says, 'You have to.' She says, very seriously, 'I can't.' He reverses his field, says, 'You can't.' Instantly she says, 'I have to.' And so on, for as long as he is willing to play.

To almost every question she answers 'No', or the negative 'Unh-unh'. This does not mean that she thinks *no* is always the correct answer; she often says *no* when she knows the correct answer is *yes*, as when her older sister, whom she loves, says, 'Are you my sister?' The word *no*, for a two-year-old, is the Declaration of Independence and Magna Charta rolled into one. Oddly enough, most people seem alarmed by the first signs of independence in small children. Modern parents often say, 'It's just a stage, they'll grow out of it,' as if it were a disease from which, with care and luck, the child might recover. The more old-fashioned ones set out to show the tiny child Who Is Boss, though the child feels completely dependent and though his desire for greater independence needs all the nourishment it can get.

Lisa, like all little children, wants to do what the big people are doing. This can make problems. At dinner, she insists that her food, like everyone else's, be served from the serving dish on to a regular plate, not specially dished out in advance. A few nights ago we were having pork chops. I knew she could not possibly cut a chop and would only eat a few bites from it, so I tried to cut off some pieces of a chop for her. She protested,

'I want meat! I want meat!' I said, 'I'm giving you meat.' No use; I knew what she wanted, and she knew I knew. An entire chop had to be put on her plate. Only after she had sawed futilely at it for a while with knife and fork ('foik'), did she allow me to cut some off for her.

She shows this independence in many ways. In the yard behind the little house are some swings, attached to the frame by chains, so that their height may be adjusted. An older child had taken off one of the swings and left it on the ground. Lisa wanted to swing on it, and was fooling around with it on the ground. I said, 'Do you want to swing on it?' she said, 'No,' but as she always says that, and as she looked as if she wanted to swing, I started to attach one of the chains to its hook. She said sternly, 'No fix swing.' She then took the other chain, and holding it by the end began to reach towards the top bar of the frame, meanwhile making earnest jumps, which took her about an inch-and-a-half off the ground. After a while she gave up and turned to something else. I moved towards the swing again. Right away she said, 'No fix swing, John.' By degrees this turned into a game. I would slowly approach the chain; she would say, 'No fix swing.' I would move away. A little later, we would go through it again. Her expression was playful, but she was serious. Not until later, when she had gone off on other business of her own, was I able to fix the swing.

Even a year ago she wanted very much to be included in any game that people were playing. Then it was easier to fool her. If the older children were playing checkers, or Parcheesi, or chess, they could generally appease and get rid of Lisa by giving her a few extra pieces to play with on the floor. But this didn't last for long. She soon saw that cards, or pieces, were being used in a particular way, and she wanted to use them that way – on the board itself. This makes it hard for the chess players. When she sees a chess game going on, or hears one mentioned, she immediately wants to play. Not that she particularly cares about the game, even as she understands it – or doesn't understand it – she just doesn't want to be excluded from what the others are doing. Sometimes her brothers try to hide the game by playing on the top bunk in their room. But she soon tracks them down, and begins to say, 'Need to play chess! Need to! Need to!' No use to give her extra pieces; she wants to play right on the board itself. We can only persuade her to let the boys finish their game by promising her a chance to play later, which she does, happily, with whoever will 'play' with her, for a long time.

Her patience and concentration are astonishing. The other day she found a green ball-point pen, and took it apart. There were four pieces: the cartridge; the two pieces that made up the body of the pen, and that had to be screwed together; and a metal band, which had to be put on one of the plastic pieces before they were screwed together. There should have been a spring, but by the time I saw the pen, it was gone. I started to put the pieces together for her, but she told me not to. She worked clumsily but patiently with the pieces, trying all possible ways of combining them. She was not sure how the pieces ought to look when fitted together, and did not have the skill to fit them; nevertheless, she came close. She often got the parts together in the proper order, but could not engage the screw threads to get the two halves of the case together. Time and time again she would seem to have the pieces put together properly, only to have them fall apart. She did not get angry or discouraged, and worked on it for more than twenty minutes, only stopping when called to lunch.

As I watched, I thought of many four-year-olds I had seen in nursery school trying to put puzzles together, and often getting tearful or angry when they could not. Why are older children so much less able to stand the frustration of – let us call it, not failure, but deferred success? I suspect it is because they are already, even in nursery school, in a very competitive, status-conscious situation, all struggling for the approval of the teacher, or each other. The child who cannot do the puzzle knows that older children have already done it, and that the teacher and other children expect him to do it, and will be disappointed or make fun of him, if he can't do it. But Lisa is still interested only in the pen, and whether she can get it together; she doesn't care whether other people can do it, or what they think of her efforts to do it. To many four-year-olds, doing a puzzle is often only a means to an end – gaining someone else's approval. To Lisa, putting the pen together is an end in itself.

22 March 1963

The other day Danny did something so exactly like what little children are supposed to do that it sounds made up. He has three picture puzzles, like jigsaw puzzles, only much simpler. Two are the Playskool variety, seen in many nursery schools. The other is a very pretty, and much more intricate and interesting Dutch puzzle. Though Danny is only 29 months old, he can put these puzzles together with no outside help. It is surprising that he should have such skilful fingers, or be able to keep three such complicated patterns in his head. He does not do these puzzles by trial and error, not any more. He *knows* where each piece in each of the puzzles goes. He has a rough order in which he likes to put the puzzles together, but he is not a prisoner of that order. At any one point there is probably a piece that he would rather put in than any other, but if that piece doesn't fall under his eye, he can use another, and place it correctly. It is quite something to watch.

The other day he was working on one of the Playskool puzzles, which is about boats. One of the pieces, which fits along an edge, is a cloud. He picked it up, took it to its proper place, and tried to fit it in. But he had turned it a little bit away from the proper angle, so that he couldn't get it to go right up to the edge. Also, there were no other pieces in place around it to guide it in. He struggled and pushed with it, turning it this way and that, but couldn't quite get it to fit. He grew more and more uneasy; he *knew* that it was supposed to go there, but it wouldn't. His movements became more rapid and anxious. Suddenly he turned away from the puzzle, crawled to his blanket, a few feet behind him, grabbed it, stuck his thumb in his mouth, and sat down on the floor, looking at us as if to say, 'I know what to do at a time like this.' We all laughed delightedly. In a moment or so he had recharged his battery enough so that he could go back to the puzzle, put in some other pieces, and soon finish it, including the piece that had caused the trouble.

7 March 1963

I had another visit with Danny. We were walking around the Visual Arts Centre at Harvard, when he looked up and saw the moon. He pointed it out to us. A moment later, after we had walked a short way up the street, he looked up and noticed it again. He seemed surprised to see it in what may have seemed to be a different place.

He talks a great deal. I notice that, when we say something to him, he will often repeat the last word or two, as if for practice.

When we got home, we invented two good games. I don't know how either of them got started. There was a small, soft cushion on the couch. For some reason, at one point, I threw it to him. He caught it, and threw it back. This was very exciting for him. I imagine that following the cushion through the air with his eyes, and timing his grab with its arrival, was a good exercise in coordination. It is also an easy game, since the cushion is soft, does not bounce away from him, and is easy to hold on to. He also has a big balloon that he likes to catch, though it behaves quite differently.

The other game was 'hit-the-bed'. When we were playing catch, I was sitting on a day bed. I felt that this little boy had more energy on hand than he could either contain or get rid of, and remembering how Lisa used to love to hit the cushion of a chair with a stick, making a noise that made her blink, I raised my hand over my head and brought it, palm down, hard as I could, on the bed, making a good, solid noise. Danny was delighted. I said to him, 'You hit the bed.' He came up and gave it a rather tentative slap. I said, 'Oh, you can hit it harder than that,' and gave it another good smack. But not until after several tries did he let go his inhibitions and hit as hard as he could.

From this beginning the game developed. During our game of catch with the pillow, every so often he would stop and say, 'Hit the bed.' Each time I hit it with all my might; each time he laughed. Then one time, for no reason, with no plan in mind, instead of hitting the bed hard, I gave it only a little pat. Then I said, 'Shall I hit it harder?' He said, 'Yes.' I hit it slightly harder, then repeated my question. Another yes. A harder blow; the same question; another yes, and so four or five times, until I was hitting it as hard as I could. We went through the cycle a couple of times. The third time, after giving the bed a light tap, I waited. He looked at me a second, then said, 'Harder!' I hit it harder, but not very. Again, 'Harder!' I put on a little more steam. Again, and louder than before, 'Harder!' And so we progressed until I hit a full-sized blow. He was delighted and excited by this game; later we played it for his parents.

The real point of the story is that the best games with little children flow easily and naturally from the situation of the moment. We are not likely to get good games by planning them far in advance, but we probably will get them if we play with children just for the fun of it. And whatever the game is, we must be ready to give it up, instantly and without regret, if the child is not enjoying it. It's tempting to think, 'If I can just get him to do this for a while, he will enjoy it.' But he won't – and we won't.

*

Danny has become so good at doing his Playskool puzzles that his parents have bought him some jigsaw puzzles. He now has two or three of these that he can put together very well. Last night he was working on one that shows a picture of a Mexican boy and two goats. It was amazing to watch him. He has some

34

picture of the completed puzzle in his mind. It tells him that this piece goes here and that piece there. He looks at the pieces for a few seconds, then suddenly reaches out, picks a piece, and puts it where he thinks it should go. Four times out of five, he is right. And when he is wrong, he usually sees very quickly that he is, and without any fuss gives up his attempt to make the piece go where it should not.

Last night there was one exception. He tried to put a piece into a spot. It was almost the right shape, and the colours matched quite well, though not exactly. It seemed clear that he does not have a feeling for an exact colour match; he doesn't do puzzles this way. The piece was just close enough to being right so that he felt it should go in. Before long he had passed the point at which he could give up the effort to make it fit. Pride, face, had become involved. You could see him getting angry, and a bit frightened, as children do when a part of the world that had been making sense suddenly stops making it. His father began trying to persuade him to consider the idea that this might be the wrong piece. He went at it very gently and tactfully. But the boy wasn't ready to admit that; he knew it was the right piece, only it just wouldn't go! After a while I had a hunch. I said, 'Why don't you put it here, outside, for a minute, and put some of the other pieces in, and then try it later. Let it alone for a minute.' This he was ready to do. He put in a few other pieces, and then took the difficult piece and without any hesitation put it into the place that had by this time become ready for it. It turned out to be next to the place where he had been trying to put it: he had not been very far wrong after all.

It seems to me that there is some kind of lesson in this for students and teachers alike. There are times when even the most skilful learner must admit to himself that for the time being he is trying to butt his head through a stone wall, and that there is no sense in it. At such times teachers are inclined to use students as a kind of human battering ram. I've done it too often myself. It doesn't work.

Danny, his parents and I went next door to visit a little girl about his age. She also had some of those Playskool puzzles, but apparently had not been able to put them together. Her way of playing with the puzzle was to take a piece, any piece at all, stick it into what was obviously an impossible place, look around, and make a kind of isn't-that-silly? giggle. Her strategy is very like that of older children and adults, a strategy of deliberate failure. If you can't play a game the way it is supposed to be played, turn it into a game that you can play. If you can't do it right, do it wrong, but so obviously wrong that everyone will see that you are not trying to do it right, and that you don't think it is worth trying to do right.

Later, back at Danny's house, he put some of his puzzles out on the floor. He had already done one, and was full of energy and confidence. Suddenly he began doing what the little girl had done earlier, putting pieces in what were clearly the wrong places, looking at me, and laughing. This was a big joke: but it was very different from the girl's self-protective, camouflage joke. He knew he could do the puzzle right, and he chose to pretend to do it wrong, just because it was funny. At first the importance of this escaped me, perhaps because we soon were doing other things. But later he was showing us one of his favourite books, about machines – construction and earthmoving machines, whose names he knew by heart, and loved to say. Then he turned to the inside cover of the book, where there were a number of Walt Disney characters. Some he knew; others he asked us. Soon he went back to the inside of the book again, but now he played a different game. At each page he would show us a machine and tell us something that the machine was *not*; thus he looked at the picture of the cement mixer and said, 'Tractor', and at the picture of the steam shovel and said, 'Combine', with great relish and enjoyment. To look at something and deliberately call it something else was a good joke.

This seems a very healthy, confident, and powerful attitude towards the world of symbols. They are ours to use as we wish. We can use them correctly if we want; but if we want to use them incorrectly, for a joke, we can do that too. We are in charge, not the symbols.

This feeling, that when you know how to do something right it is often fun to do it wrong, is strong in children. Adults who meet it tend to discourage it. I think this is a mistake, perhaps a serious one, and that the kind of thing I saw my little friend doing the other night should be enjoyed and encouraged. It is not always necessary to be right.

Children can learn some cause-and-effect games when they are very young. When I was last in France, I was visiting a young schoolteacher and his family. Their boy was less than a year-and-a-half old. I often used to watch him in his crib, talk to him, play with him. One of his toys was a rubber ring, about the size of a deck-tennis ring, slightly bigger than a doughnut. One day, as he watched, I put it on top of my head. After a second or two I nodded my head and the ring slid down over my face and fell. Then I put the ring on his head. He did the same thing. This turned into a good game. After we each had had several turns I put the ring on my head and waited. He watched me for a few seconds; then he made an insistent ducking motion with his head. I ducked my head, and the ring fell off. He was delighted, and we did this over and over again.

Once, years before, with a still younger child, not more than seven or eight months old, I played the game of 'Bump'. I was carrying her around, and for some reason, I forget what, we bumped heads gently. I said, 'Bump'. She seemed to enjoy the incident, so I said, 'Bump' again, and again bumped my forehead lightly against hers. After a few times, she understood the game, and when I said, 'Bump', would bump her forehead against mine – and then give me a huge smile.

1 May 1960

A few days ago, about forty minutes before regular classes started, I took my electric portable typewriter into the three-year-olds' classroom. When I went in, I didn't say anything, just went over to a corner of the room, set the machine up on a low table, and, very slowly, one finger at a time, began to type. For a while the children circled warily at a distance, now and then, in the middle of their play, casting quick glances at me out of the corners of their eyes. Gradually the bolder children came closer and closer. Finally, as I had hoped, one of them came up close and asked if he could do it. I said, 'Sure, if you want to.' Before long they all wanted a turn. While one typed, the others crowded around the machine, pushing silently and insistently, like people waiting for a train. The typewriter was almost too popular. I couldn't let any one child type for even as long as five minutes, which wasn't enough time for them to do much investigating and exploring, let alone discovering. Also, the child working with the machine was more than a little distracted by the excitement of the other children.

9 May 1960

The three-year-olds continue to be fascinated with the typewriter. John is usually one of the first to come in each morning. As soon as he sees me, he asks for a turn. He also likes to plug in the machine. On about the fourth day with the machine, he said to me as I left to go to my own class, 'Mr Holt, you have to bring the typewriter over to my house.' Two others then said the same thing

On the fifth day John discovered the gadget that changes the ribbon from red to black, and noticed that it made a difference in the colours that came out on the paper. By now all the veterans know about this gadget and like to work it. They are beginning to be slightly more interested in the marks made on the paper, instead of just running the machine for the sake of making it go. They might be even more interested if the letters made by the typewriter were bigger.

Elsie (aged five-and-a-half), sister of Charlie, had a turn. She can read and spell. She wrote, without help, DEAR DADDY, I LOVE YOU AND YOUR ROOM. This excited and aroused Matt (four). He wanted to write something to his father. I showed him what keys to hit to make DEAR DADDY. He wrote DDEAR DDADDY. But this was all he could think of to say. Perhaps the slowness of having to hunt for the letters made his thinking freeze up. He was torn between his desire to make the machine go lickety-split, and his desire to make it say something.

Charlie (just four years old), unlike most of these kids, wants to know what the letters are as he hits them. He is deliberate, hits one key at a time, and looks at the mark he has made. Perhaps, in time, he might lead the group to new discoveries. One day, looking down through the keyboard, he noticed the spinning bar inside the machine – the one that moves the keys. He was eager to find out what it was.

On about the sixth day Matt, looking at the letters and numerals on the paper, suddenly said, 'There's the number five!' He was very excited to see something he recognized.

When the children first started using the machine, they would type up to the end of a line and then go on typing, not noticing that nothing was happening. After a while I started saying, when we reached the end of a line, 'End of the line!' before returning the carriage. By now they all know how to use the carriage return, and when to use it; I hardly ever have to say 'End of the line' anymore. Charlie likes to say it himself each time he returns the carriage.

A few of the children have become skilful and surprisingly gentle at untangling stuck keys.

Some days later Matt wanted to write FATHER. I wrote it for him on a piece of paper. He found the F and the A on the keyboard by himself; I showed him the others. Then he found a most ingenious way to satisfy his desire to make the machine go fast as well as his desire to use it to say something. He wrote: FFFFFFFAAAAAAATTTTTTTHHHHHHHEEEEEEERRRRRRR.

Charlie can find, and likes to find, the C with which his name begins. When I asked whether he could find the other letters, he gave me an anxious look, so I quickly let the matter drop. How strongly and immediately children react to being put on this kind of spot. He likes to have me name the keys that he hits. He knows that in the top row the numeral keys are followed by a dash and then the equals sign, and he often remembers to say 'dash' and 'equals' even when I don't.

For much of the year, when I entered the room, John has told me that he was the sheriff and that I would have to go to jail. I thought of the success that Sylvia Ashton-Warner had had, teaching her children words that they really were excited about. So one day I wrote, in large capitals on a sheet of paper, GO TO JAIL. I showed it to John and told him what it said. I thought he might be interested in writing it on the typewriter. So much for bright ideas – he couldn't have cared less. He then asked me to write, with pencil, GO HOME; but to my surprise, he showed no interest in writing any of those letters on the typewriter. However, he still gets angry if other children write J, which he claims is *his* letter.

2 April 1961

The other afternoon Scott, who will be six in a few months, was fooling around with the electric typewriter. Like most of the five-year-olds who have used it in class this year, he has looked on it, first of all, as a machine to make go and, secondly, as a device for making many marks on a sheet of paper. He has not looked on it as an easy way of writing, that is, saying something. On the other hand, he doesn't look on any kind of writing as a way of saying something. Writing, for him and his classmates, is a way of making certain kinds of marks, which the adults seem to like, with a pencil or crayon. It has nothing to do with getting speech on to paper.

At any rate, he had the shift lock depressed and was happily making patterns of dollar signs. By mistake he released the shift lock, so that he began to get, instead of dollar signs, a row of 4s. He didn't like this, and said so. Then he went about trying to get his dollar signs back. With much audible muttering of 'Let's try this', he pressed first one unmarked key and then another, getting various unexpected and unwanted results, until he finally hit the shift lock and the missing dollar sign was restored, to his great satisfaction.

His teacher later said that there was a noticeable difference between the 'bright' kids in the class and the less 'bright', in that the bright ones made a very deliberate use of the scientific method, the selective use of trial and error. Not only did they use this as a way of finding out what they wanted to know, but they were conscious of using it. The question is, do they use the method because they are bright, or is it the use of the method that makes them bright?

In the last year or two I have seen a good deal of Tommy, Lisa's little brother. He too is a tireless and resourceful experimenter. When he was two-and-a-half, he liked to plug the vacuum cleaner into the electric socket, so that he could hear the motor start. Since no amount of threats and punishment seemed to keep him away from plugs, and since the house is full of them, we decided the best thing to do was concentrate on making sure that he used plugs correctly – which he did. Like most children, he is eager to learn to do things the right way.

One day, as I watched him plug in the vacuum cleaner, I brought over the end of the suction pipe, which had no attachments on it, and invited him to feel the end of the pipe. He was surprised to find his hand sucked hard against it. He liked this, and did it over and over. This added a new dimension to his experiment. Now, each time he put in the plug, he would feel the end of the pipe.

I felt, watching him do this, that for a while he was not sure each time, whether his hand would be sucked or not. Just because it happened once did not necessarily mean that it would happen again. It takes children some time to learn that, in many cases, a particular event A will always be followed by some other event B, and that if B follows A once, you can count on it to do so again.

One day he was happily plugging and unplugging the vacuum cleaner and testing the suction with his hand. Suddenly he looked thoughtfully at pipe and plug. He had an idea. Very deliberately he brought the end of the pipe over to the socket, and then with his other hand felt the plug! He seemed surprised to feel no suction. He repeated the experiment a time or two, again without results. Then he went back to his original game. It is hard not to feel that the experiment he had done showed a kind of mental skill that one would not expect in a two-and-a-half-year-old.

Yet there are odd limitations to what little children can do. The following summer, at age three, he was dragging one of his favourite toys – the garden hose – around the yard. Suddenly the hose, which was looped around a small cottonwood sapling that we had planted not long before, came up taut, and he could pull no further. It seemed easy enough to see what was happening; the tree wasn't far away from him. But he just pulled harder and harder, getting frustrated and angry. Finally he asked for help, and I led him and the hose around the tree, thus freeing him. I think he would have understood the hose being caught if something heavy had been lying on it. But he could not imagine that anything as static and passive as a tree could be causing the trouble.

*

Tommy, too, has had his turn at the typewriter. I was typing one day in the living room, when he came in and saw me. He wanted a turn, so I put him on a chair before me and he started. Right away he surprised me. He is a very bold, energetic, exuberant little boy. I thought he might begin to bang on the keys, like other three-year-olds I have known. But no – he hit them quite carefully, and deliberately, one at a time. Is it too far-fetched to think that, living in a family where many people understand machines and can fix them, he has a kind of respect for machines?

Like all little children, he was fascinated with the typewriter, first of all, as a machine, something to make go. He made a move; it made a move. Like other small children, he looked intently at each key he hit. Only once in a while did he look at the paper to see the mark he had made; when he did look, he did not look carefully to see *what* mark had been made, much less compare it with the letter he had hit. This might have come in time, but we never got to that point. On the other hand, like most children, he was interested in the names of at least some of the letters he was hitting. Very soon, he asked me where O was. I showed him. I also told him the names of some other letters he hit, though not all of them, and not all the time. After a while he asked me where E was, and where A was. Had he known them before he heard me mention them? I don't know. I showed him where they were, and it was only a very short time before he knew where all three of these letters were on the keyboard. He would say, 'Where O is?' I would say, 'Where do you think?' He would point to it.

This game was fun. But it was not as much fun as we adults tend to think, and he quickly invented a variation of it. He would ask where O, (or A, or E) was; I would show him, and he would say, 'That's not O' (or A, or E). There was a trace of exasperation in his tone. Then he would point to some other letter – remember that he *had* been able to point to O in the first place – and say that *it* was O. I would say, 'No that's U' (or whatever it was). He did not insist; but he did this many times. I was puzzled what to make of it. Remembering Lisa at the same age, I guessed that this might be his way of resisting and reacting to a situation in which I was in control and had *all* the information, *all* the right answers. He was asserting himself, and his right to make some of the rules. I don't think he liked the idea that O *had* to be where I said it was. Though I doubt if he had any such conscious and definite thought in mind, I think he felt that if I could name letters, why couldn't he? Why didn't he have as much right as I to say where O was?

He insisted on being allowed to put the paper into the machine. In this he was unusual among the small children I have worked with. It was a tricky job. Unless you get the paper all the way in to where the rollers grip it, nothing happens when you try to turn the platen (the roller against which you type). He often found himself in this jam. When he had turned a while without anything happening, he would let me push the paper down far enough for the rollers to engage it; but he had to have his chance to do it first. The next problem was that the paper would go in crooked. I could usually say, 'Here, let me straighten that out a bit,' and do so. Then the paper would come up in front of the type, and get caught on the bar that holds it firmly against the platen. For the first few times this happened, I would lift up the bar and push the paper under it; after that, he was able to do it for himself.

At one point he asked to see 'the noise'. By this he meant the electric motor, which could be heard humming away inside. I said, 'Do I really have to take it all the way out of its case?' He insisted; so I did. He looked at the motor, touched it. He looked as if he would like to take it out altogether. I don't remember any other child ever asking to see the motor before – but he comes from a very mechanical family.

It was near the very end of my visit that we began working with the typewriter. In the short time we did work, he showed little or no desire to learn the names of letters other than O, A, and E. Now and then he would ask the names of other letters, but not often, and he seemed not to remember them. I had the feeling that what he wanted to find out about this machine was how to operate it, and once he felt he knew that, there was not much more of importance to learn. Perhaps, with more time, he would have become interested in what the machine was doing.

*

What Tommy really liked to work was the player piano. It began with watching his older sister, Lisa, work it. She plays it often for the sake of the music. He wanted to play it because she does, as he wants to do everything she can do. He could barely reach the pedals, and had to work like a Trojan to make them go. To keep himself in the piano stool, he had to hold the edge of the piano with both hands. But then the stool, sitting on a hardwood floor, would begin to slide away from the piano. After a while, it would gradually slide him out of reach. He would have to get off, move the stool back, get back on, and begin again. Once, watching this, I said, 'Here, I'll hold the stool,' and did so. This worked fine, but now I had a permanent job. From then on, every time he wanted to play, I would hear his piercing voice: 'John! John!' If I was doing something else, and didn't want to stop, I would lie low; but that was never much good. Eventually he would track me down and say, 'Peash help me.' It was impossible to resist. I would ask, knowing what he wanted, 'What do you want me to do?' He would say, 'Hold that tool.' Off we would go.

He was mainly interested in the piano as a machine, something to make go. When he began, we thought that if he tried to put in the piano roll, he would tear it. So we told him to let one of the older people put it in. At first he didn't mind: there were many other things in and on the piano to think about. But after a while he found that this meant that he couldn't play unless he could first hunt up someone to put in a roll, which was a nuisance. Also, he saw other people putting in the roll, so why couldn't he?

In Tommy's family, when a machine breaks down, someone in the family instantly tears it apart and fixes it. His father has always been an expert mechanic, and the feeling that machines can be fixed by anyone has been absorbed by the older boys, who as a matter of routine take bikes, automobiles, or anything else apart and put them together again. So when anything is broken, the little boy expects someone to 'fit it'. His first instinct, faced with a machine, like the player piano, is to dive into its innards and see how everything works.

Before long he learned how to put in a piano roll, and to work all the other controls. There is a lever to adjust the side-to-side position of the roll, and another to adjust the tempo. He worked them both, though I don't know if he could gauge the results he was getting. Another lever reversed the roll, to rewind it. Still another, under the keyboard, made a change in the tone of the piano, giving it a twangier sound. He found all these levers, and used all of them. In fact, for him, playing the piano meant operating every control in sight.

After a while he asked me what the lever was for that moved the roll from side to side. I showed him the holes in the paper, and how they moved over a brass perforated rod, which in turn made the piano play. Did he understand everything I said? I don't know, or care. From then on, it was a part of his piano-playing routine to climb up on the stool, inspect some of the holes in the roll, say, 'Hole all right,' and get down again to go on playing. I guess I had once said that the holes were all right to discourage him from examining them; if I was going to have to hold the stool for him while he played, I wanted him to play, not inspect. But it didn't work out that way. He remembered my remark, and made the hole inspection a regular part of his playing.

It makes me think how much children must have learned from watching people do real work, in the days when a child could see people doing real work. It is not so easy to manage this now. So much of the so-called work done in our society is not work at all, certainly not as a child could understand it; so much of the rest is done by machines. But there are still plenty of craftsmen, of all kinds. What a good thing it would be if a way could be found for many children to see them at their work, and to be able to ask them questions about it.

Back to the player piano. Some of the controls I have mentioned are underneath a little hinged strip of wood at the edge of the keyboard. Once, when he started to play, again with the idea of discouraging him from fooling too much with the controls, I closed this hinged cover, saying, 'Let's get this out of the way.' This too became part of his regular routine. Every so often, when playing, he would close this cover and say, 'Get this out of the way.'

Thus children learn that certain phrases go along with certain actions, fit into certain situations. Is this use of language imitative? To some extent. But it is not on that account blind or purposeless imitation. A real connexion has been found, and is used. Also, the child soon joins the phrase, 'Get this out of the way,' to the act of getting the thing out of the way, and knows that the one means the other. The question would be, how soon can he use the same phrase in a different context? Perhaps he may have to hear it used in another context before he realizes that it can fit, not just one situation, but many.

Another thing he learned to do was fold back the pedals and close the doors, thus making the piano into a regular piano. He also liked to work the sliding doors that covered the roll mechanism. At one point, watching the piano keys move up and down as he pumped the pedals, he got the idea of holding on to one of the keys, to see what would happen, to find out, perhaps, how strong was the force moving them. Fearing he might break something, I prevented this contest of strength.

He also liked to turn the crank that raises and lowers the grill on the outdoor charcoal grill. Now and then he lowered it all the way and since he kept on turning, backed the crank out of the screw threads, so that it came loose. When this happened, he tried to screw the crank back. Some kinds of screws he can thread, but this one was too tricky for him. Usually, after trying a while, he left the handle on the ground, or carried it around a while before leaving it. We learned to recognize it, even in odd places, and to take it back to the grill. We let the game go on, because it is a good and valuable game. To crank a handle one way, and see that something goes up, and then to crank it the other way, and see the thing go down, is an interesting and important experiment for a small child. He not only learns how this particular crank works; he also learns that many actions have regular and predictable effects, and that the world is in many ways a sensible and trustworthy place.

About a year after all these experiments took place, his mother wrote me, in part:

He is the most *noticing*, thoughtful, quick little boy and he hates to be *taught*. He loves to learn things and stores up all sorts of facts for future use. He uses his tools (screwdriver, hammer, spade and rake, saw, etc.) with great skill and care. He loves to do things *with* us – he plants and waters for me – clips the grass – strains sand for cement, etc. – is busy and curious. But when we try (as we are now) to *teach* him something like *ABCDEFG*, which appears to be without meaning or use he just can't *bear* it – in fact he becomes furious and frustrated – almost in tears. How will he react to school this fall?

Lisa is a super-serious student – she now has an all A report card and really *worries* about her grades. She *hates* to be unprepared for school and yet she really deeply dislikes it . . .

14 October 1963

The other day, I brought to school an old army bugle that I had bought second-hand for eight dollars. When the first-grade and kindergarten children went out to recess, I took the bugle out. I gave it a tentative *blat* or two (I can't play it), and about 20 children crowded around me, clamouring for a turn. I lined them up, and off we went. Quite a number of them knew, from having watched me, what to do with their lips. Others put the whole mouthpiece in their mouths, like a lollipop, before realizing that that wouldn't work. Then they tried it the right way. Some I had to show, pursing my lips and blowing through them, what had to be done. Nine out of ten children were able to get a good sound – that is, a strong sound – out of the bugle. Some could make as much noise on it as I could. They got tremendous pleasure and satisfaction from it – particularly Martin. I could hardly get it away from him. And a few, sad, defeated little children would come up, give a weak puff through the instrument, and hand it back to me with a resigned expression. Why did these few give up so easily?

After about four days of this, one of the teachers came out – from her coffee break – and said to please stop playing the bugle, it made her too nervous. So that was the end of that. But it was interesting to see, if only for a short while, how energetically and confidently most of these little children tackled the problem of getting a sound out of a difficult instrument.

8 November 1963

On days when I have a lesson, I bring my cello to school, take it to a classroom, and give the children a turn at 'playing' it. Except for the timid ones, who make a few half-hearted passes with the bow and then quit, almost all little children attack the cello in the same way. They are really doing three things at once: they are making the machine go; they are enjoying the luxury of making sounds; and they are making scientific experiments. They start off by working the bow vigorously back and forth across one of the strings. They keep this up for a long time. Just the feel and sound of it are exciting. Then they begin to vary their bowing a bit, trying different rhythms. After a while, they begin to move the bow so that it touches more than one string, or they move to another string. But it is important to note that the first few times they do this, they do not seem to be doing it in the spirit of an experiment, to find out what will happen. They do it for the sake of doing it. They have been bowing one way, making one kind of noise; now they want to bow another way, and make another kind of noise. Only after some time does it seem to occur to them that there was a relation between the way they bowed and the kind of noise they got. Then there is quite a change in their way of doing things. This time they move more deliberately, watchfully, thoughtfully, from one string to another. You can almost hear them thinking, 'Ah, this string makes this kind of noise, and that string makes that kind of noise.' But they have to do a good deal of what seems like random bowing, activity for its own sake, before they begin to think about what they are doing. They have to pile up quite a mass of raw sensory data before they begin trying to sort it out and make sense of it.

After they have done a good deal of bowing they begin to think about using the fingers of their left hand to press the strings down on the fingerboard. This does not have much effect, for two reasons. In the first place, their fingers are not

49

strong enough to hold the strings down tightly enough. More important, they do not at first make the slightest effort to be sure they are holding down the same string they are bowing. The bow works furiously across all the strings. The left hand goes up and down the strings, pressing them here and there, but the two activities are not connected. While this goes on, I say nothing. After a while, the child begins to be aware of something. What? Perhaps his left hand becomes aware, so to speak, of holding down a vibrating string some of the time, and a silent string the rest of the time. Perhaps he becomes aware that some of the time his left hand affects the sound, and some of the time it does not. At any rate, after a while he begins to make a deliberate effort to hold down the same string he is bowing on, looking from one hand to the other. This is harder than it looks, especially for a little child holding the cello in a very awkward position. When he gets the hang of it, he bows away some more, pressing down here and there on the bowed string, again in what seems like a random, undirected way, for some time, before he begins to conduct a series of new experiments, this time to see what happens when he moves his hand up and down the string.

It doesn't take a child long, by such steps, to grasp the basic idea of the cello, the relationship of the bow, the string, and the left hand. But while he has been figuring this out, he has been ceaselessly active. One could say that he is having too much fun – a weak word, really – playing the cello to want to take time to figure it out. A scientist might say that, along with his useful data, the child has collected an enormous quantity of random, useless data. A trained scientist wants to cut all irrelevant data out of his experiment. He is asking nature a question, and he wants to cut down the noise, the static, the random information, to a minimum, so that he can hear the answer. But a child doesn't work that way. He is used to getting his answers *out of* the noise. He has, after all, grown up in a strange world where everything is noise, where he can only understand and make sense of a tiny part of what he experiences. His way of attacking the cello problem is to produce the maximum amount of data possible, to do as many things as he can, to use his hands and the bow in as many ways as possible. Then, as he goes along, he begins to notice regularities and patterns. He begins to ask questions – that is, to make deliberate experiments. But it is vital to note that until he has a great deal of data, he has no idea what questions to ask, or what questions there are to be asked.

There is a special sense in which it may be fair to say that the child scientist is a less efficient thinker than the adult scientist. He is not as good at cutting out unnecessary and useless information, at simplifying the problem, at figuring out how to ask questions whose answers will give him the most information. Thus, a trained adult thinker, seeing a cello for the first time, would probably do in a few seconds what it takes a child much longer to do – bow each of the strings to see what sounds they give, and then see what effect holding down a string with the left hand has on the sound made by that string. That is, if – and it is a very big if – he could bring himself to touch the cello at all. Where the young child, at least until his thinking has been spoiled by adults, has a great advantage is in situations – and many, even most, real-life situations are like this – where there is so much seemingly senseless data that it is impossible to tell what questions to ask. He is much better at taking in this kind of data; he is better able to tolerate its confusion; and he is much better at picking out the patterns, hearing the faint signal amid all the noise. Above all, he is much less likely than adults to make hard and fast conclusions on the basis of too little data, or having made such conclusions, to refuse to consider any new data that does not support them. And these are the vital skills of thought which, in our hurry to get him thinking the way we do, we may very well stunt or destroy in the process of 'educating' him.

Talk

Sitting in his stroller, in a local store the other day, was a child about a year old. His mother was busy in the store, and he was absorbed in his own affairs, playing with his stroller, looking at cans of fruit and juice. I watched him. Suddenly he said to himself, 'Beng-goo.' After a few seconds he said it again, then again, and so perhaps ten times. Was he trying to say, 'Thank you'? More probably he had hit on this sound by accident and was saying it over and over because he liked the way it sounded, and felt in his mouth.

A few months ago, I saw quite a bit of another one-year-old. She liked to say, 'Leedle-leedle-leedle-leedle.' It was her favourite sound, and she said it all the time; indeed that was about all she said. Now and then she would add an emphatic 'a!' (as in cat) – 'Leedle-leedle-leedle-a!' I asked her father how she had come to make that sound. Was she imitating a sound that someone had made to her? No; apparently she had learned to stick her tongue out and bring it back in quickly, and liked the feel of it. (Babies like all tongue-waggling games.) One day, as she was doing this, she made a sound with her voice, and was amazed and delighted to hear what the movement of her tongue did to that sound. After much practice she found that she could make the sound without having to put her tongue outside her mouth. It felt good, and it sounded good, so she kept it up for a month or two before moving on to something else.

How a sound feels seems to be as important as the sound itself. Everyone who has watched babies knows how pleased they are when they first discover how to make a Bronx cheer. And they do discover it; this sound, at least, is one that their mother would never teach them.

In France, some years ago, I was surprised to hear an eighteen-month-old boy, while babbling away, make the sound of the French 'u'. Perhaps there was no reason to be surprised; everyone who talked to him called him *'tu'*. But I had never heard a baby make that sound before, and had had a very hard time to get even a few of my French students to make it. Of course, my students were anxious and self-conscious, and this baby was not – which makes a world of difference.

Why does a baby begin to make sounds in the first place? Is it instinctive, like crying? It seems not to be. A puppy raised apart from other dogs will know how to bark when he gets old enough. But the few children we know of who grew up without human contact, grew up almost wholly mute. Babies in under-staffed foundling hospitals, who see very little of older people, are said, except for crying, to be almost silent. Apparently it is from hearing people speak around them that babies get the idea of 'speaking'. When they make their first sounds, are they imitating the sounds they hear around them? Or are they inventing, so to speak, from scratch? Perhaps at first they mostly invent, and imitate more later.

It is a remarkable business. We are so used to talking that we forget that it takes a very subtle and complicated coordination of lips, tongue, teeth, palate, jaws, cheeks, voice, and breath. Simply as a muscular skill it is by far the most complicated and difficult that most of us ever learn, at least as difficult as the skill required to master a serious musical instrument. We realize how difficult speech is only when we first try to make the sounds of a language very different from our own. Suddenly we find out that our mouths and tongues won't do what we want. Yet every child learns to make the sounds of his own language. If he lives where more than one language is spoken, he makes the sounds of them all. How does he do it? His coordination is poor to start with; how does he manage to do what many adults find so difficult?

The answer seems to be by patient and persistent experiment; by trying many thousands of times to make sounds, syllables, and words; by comparing his own sounds to the sounds made by people around him; and by gradually bringing his own sounds closer to the others; above all, by being willing to do things wrong even while trying his best to do them right.

*

Bill Hull once said to me, 'If we taught children to speak, they'd never learn.' I thought at first he was joking. By now I realize that it was a very important truth. Suppose we decided that we had to 'teach' children to speak. How would we go about it? First, some committee of experts would analyse speech and break it down into a number of separate 'speech skills'. We would probably say that, since speech is made up of sounds, a child must be taught to make all the sounds of his language before he can be taught to speak the language itself. Doubtless we would list these sounds, easiest and commonest ones first, harder and rarer ones next. Then we would begin to teach infants these sounds, working our way down the list. Perhaps, in order not to 'confuse' the child – 'confuse' is an evil word to many educators – we would not let the child hear much ordinary speech, but would only expose him to the sounds we were trying to teach.

Along with our sound list, we would have a syllable list and a word list.

When the child had learned to make all the sounds on the sound list, we would begin to teach him to combine the sounds into syllables. When he could say all the syllables on the syllable list, we would begin to teach him the words on our word list. At the same time, we would teach him the rules of grammar, by means of which he could combine these newly-learned words into sentences. Everything would be planned with nothing left to chance; there would be plenty of drill, review, and tests, to make sure that he had not forgotten anything.

Suppose we tried to do this; what would happen? What would happen, quite simply, is that most children, before they got very far, would become baffled, discouraged, humiliated, and fearful, and would quit trying to do what we asked them. If, outside of our classes, they lived a normal infant's life, many of them would probably ignore our 'teaching' and learn to speak on their own. If not, if our control of their lives was complete (the dream of too many educators), they would take refuge in deliberate failure and silence, as so many of them do when the subject is reading.

*

Last summer, in a supermarket, a young mother came with her baby to the meat counter, and began to discuss with him, in the most lively and natural way, what meat they should get for supper. This piece of meat looked nice, but it was too expensive – terrible what was happening to food prices. This piece might be all right, but it would take too long to cook; they had many other errands to do and would not get home before four o'clock. These chops looked good, but they had had them just two nights ago. And so on. There was nothing forced or affected in her words or her voice; she might have been talking to someone her own age.

A year or more ago, some friends and I dropped in on some people who had a six-month-old baby. She was well-rested and happy, so they brought her in to see the visitors. We all admired her before going on with our talk. She was fascinated by this talk. As each person spoke, she would turn and look intently at him. From time to time she would busy herself with a toy in her lap; then after a few minutes she would begin watching and listening again. She seemed to be learning, not just that people talk, but that they talk to each other, and respond to each other's talk with smiles, and laughter, and more talk; in short, that talk is not just a kind of noise, but messages, communication.

Babies and young children like to hear adult conversation, and will often sit quietly for a long time, just to hear it. If we want to help little children as they learn to talk, one way to do it is by talking to them – provided we do it naturally and unaffectedly – and by letting them be around when we talk to other people.

*

For the first few years of her life, Lisa grew up on a cattle ranch. When she was about eighteen months old, she pointed at some cattle one day and said, 'See cows, see cows.' We were very pleased; these were about the first real words we had heard her say. We agreed that there were indeed cows out there, and said other things about them. But a few days later, going by a field with some horses in it, she said again, 'See cows.' Later, passing some sheep, she said the same thing. This was puzzling. Surely she didn't think they were all the same animal. Yet, if she knew the horses and sheep were different, why did she call them cows? Or, if she thought all animals were called 'cows', why didn't she call the family dog and cats 'cows'. Apparently, out of all the many things she saw, heard, and felt, she had isolated a group, a class, that we would call 'large animals in the fields', and to this class she had given the name 'cows'. We did not correct her, but just went on talking about cows, horses, and sheep in a normal way. Before long she divided her class of animals in the fields into sub-groups, and put the proper label on each one.

At about this time she was given a stuffed toy horse. Soon afterwards I was with her in a store full of many kinds of stuffed toy animals. To my surprise, she called them all 'horse'. But it was soon clear that here again she had created a class of things in her mind, in this case, animal toys, and given them the name 'horse' that people used to talk about her own toy. Before long, just by listening to other people talk, she realized that this class, too, was made up of sub-classes, each with its own label – dogs, cats, teddy bears, and so on. Soon she had those names well in hand.

Another child, a boy, who also grew up on a ranch, was very interested in the tractor – large, red, and noisy. One of the first words he spoke was 'tracker'. We soon realized that he applied it to an entire class of objects that we might label 'large moving machinery'. Cars, buses, trucks, steam shovels, bulldozers, road graders, cranes – all were 'trackers'. But before long, just by listening to other people's talk, he saw that this class had sub-groups, each with its own name. In time, like most small boys, he knew the name of every kind of machine in the neighbourhood.

This feat of naming things is more remarkable than it may at first seem. When I began to work in Bill Hull's fifth grade, he used to have the students play a game called 'categories'. He would give them a word, say 'bean'. Their task was then to find into what categories a bean could fit. They could say that it was an object, a plant, a living thing, a food, a vegetable, green, something to cook, and so on. Most of the children saw in time that any object, such as a bean, could be considered a member of a large number of classes of things. When we talk about a bean, we are picking out for our attention one or more of the classes of which we consider it a member. If we are gardeners, we may think of the bean as a vine that has to have something to climb on. If we are cooks, we will think about what has to be done to prepare it for cooking, how long it takes to cook, and so on. Thus, when we name an object, we put it into a class of things that are like it, at least in certain respects, and to all of which we give the same name. This is the same procedure that Lisa used when she gave the same name to all the large animals she saw out in the fields.

But babies, when they first look at the world, do not see it this way at all. For some time they see just a mass of shifting shapes and colours, a single, ever-changing picture in front of them. The Museum of Modern Art in New York has a kind of action picture in which rotating, curved mirrors throw coloured lights on a screen in continuously changing patterns. Some people find it disturbing to watch; they keep looking for some kind of system or regularity in the pattern, and cannot find any. The world must look something like this to a baby. The picture he sees before him is not made up, as it is for us, of many separate elements, each of which we can imagine and name, by itself, and all of which we can combine in our minds in other ways. When we see a chair in a room, we can easily imagine that chair in another part of the room, or in another room, or by itself. But for the baby the chair is an integral part of the room he sees. This may be the reason, or one of the reasons, why, when we hide something from a very young baby, it ceases to exist for him. And this in turn may be one of the reasons why peek-a-boo games are such fun for small babies to play, and may contribute much to their growing understanding of the world.

A perceptive psychologist, Dr Herman Witkin, in a book called *Psychological Differentiation*, aptly described the world of the young baby as 'undifferentiated'. It can't be broken down into parts. But as a baby gets older, he begins to see the room as a collection of things that are separate. Each object in the room – chair, lamp, table – has its own existence. It can be thought about by itself. When a baby makes this step, he is said to make an ideal or mental model of the world that is differentiated.

Before he can start naming things, say a chair, the baby must take one more mental step. Not only must he see, first, that this chair exists by and of itself, independent of the room, that it could be somewhere else in the room, or in another room, he must also see that this chair is like certain other objects in the room and in other rooms. He must see that this chair is more like *that* chair than either of them are like a lamp, or a table, or a rug. Wendell Johnson, in *People in Quandaries*, put it neatly when he said that a similarity is a difference that doesn't make any difference. So the baby must see that, in spite of differences between one chair and another, they are in essential respects the same. In short, he sees that the chair is one of a family or class of like things. Only then is he ready to call such a thing a 'chair', or to understand what other people mean when they call it that. He must create the class in his mind before he can name it. Thus naming things is not just blind imitation; it is a creative act of the mind.

One day, when Danny (mentioned earlier) was very small, I was watching him play. He had not really begun to talk; there were only half-a-dozen or so 'words' that he could say. At this time he was much interested in a big alarm clock. He liked to watch it, listen to its tick, and fiddle with its knobs and levers. Seeing the clock on the mantelpiece, he began to make an insistent, one-syllable noise, which he kept on making until someone gave him the clock. It seemed clear that he was not just saying 'clock', or some baby equivalent of 'clock'. What he was saying was, 'I want that clock, I need that clock, give me that clock!'

Long before I got into teaching, I met Jackie, about two years old, who had created in his mind a class of objects that we would call 'dry, crumbly things to eat' – cookies, crackers, dry toast – to which he had given the name 'Zee'. Neither his father or mother knew how he had come to pick that word. They assured me that he had not picked up the name from them – *they* never called crackers 'Zee'. Clearly the baby had decided for himself that it was a good name for this class of things.

When Tommy was about two, he met his first horses. One of them was named Duke, the other Blueberry. They made a great impression on him, and from their names he invented his own word for horses in general – dukeberries. His family was delighted and often (not always) used the word themselves.

Some of Tommy's first words were not names of things, but other kinds of words. When he was still little enough to be carried around a good deal of the time, he used to show where he wanted to go to whoever was carrying him by pointing his hand in the desired direction and saying, imperiously, 'Way!' When he said this to me, I used to answer, 'Way,' and then add, using my language, 'Shall we go over this way?' Another of his early words was 'Down'. If he was being carried, 'Down' meant 'Put me down.' If he wasn't being carried, 'Down' meant 'Pick me up.' His old sister, when she was very little, had invented a word, 'Tup-tup', which meant exactly the same thing.

These special, non-name words that children invent remind me of something I once read or heard about the life of Victor the Wolf-boy, so called because for most of the first ten years or so of his life, as far as anyone knew, he lived isolated from all other humans. When he was found, a French doctor tried to train and teach him. He was able to domesticate him to a certain extent, to get him to wear clothes and do simple tasks, but though he tried very patiently, he was never able to teach him to speak. At one point the doctor came close to what we now call a breakthrough, and perhaps, if he had understood as much as we now think we do about the beginnings of speech, he might have been able to make better use of his opportunity.

He had been trying without success to teach Victor to make sounds stand for objects. One day Victor was hot, hungry, and thirsty. On the kitchen table was a pitcher of cold milk, all frosty on the outside. Seeing it, Victor began to make a single insistent sound which he repeated over and over. The doctor assumed that this sound meant 'milk'; at any rate, he tried thereafter to make it stand for 'milk'. What Victor meant it to stand for, more probably, was something stronger and more complicated – the feeling of being hot and thirsty, of seeing something he knew would taste wonderful and wanting it. Perhaps, had the doctor tried to make that sound stand for 'hungry and thirsty', he might have got somewhere. As it was, the wolf-boy never was able to grasp the fundamental idea and purpose of speech.

*

One day, when Tommy was very little, he decided that he needed to find out the names for a lot of things. He suddenly began to look very intently at various objects in the room, pointing out to me each of them in turn. At first I had no idea what he wanted. I thought he was asking me to give him whatever he was looking at, or to do something with it. But he showed me that that was not what he wanted. For a while I was baffled. Then, on a hunch, I tried telling him the name of what he was showing me. Instantly he showed by his expression that I had guessed right. He began to point to many other objects. Here I thought it might help if I gave him a question that he could ask whenever he wanted to know the name of something (a very useful thing also in studying a foreign language). So when he pointed to a vase, I said, 'What's that called?

That's called a vase.' I hoped that if I said it often enough, he would learn to say it. For a short while, at least, he did, but I don't know how long it stuck, or for that matter how long lasting was his need to be told the names of things. For after all, any observant child, in a family where people do much talking, soon learns what things are called just by listening to what people say about them.

I was careful, when I told him the name of something, not to tell him as if it were a lesson, something he *had* to remember. Nor did I test him by saying, 'What's this? What's that?' This kind of checking up is not necessary, and it puts a child in a spot where he will feel that, if he says the wrong thing, he has done wrong and is in the wrong. I have seen kindly, well-meaning parents do this to young children, hoping to help them learn. Almost every time the child soon took on the kind of tense, tricky expression we see on so many children's faces in school, and began the same sad old business of bluffing, guessing, and playing for hints. Even in the rare case when a child does not react this defensively to questions, too much quizzing is likely to make him begin to think that learning does not mean figuring out how things work, but getting and giving answers that please grown-ups.

We should also remember that children (like adults), and above all young children, know and understand much more than they can put into words. If we point to a lamp and say to a young child, 'What's that?' we may not always get an answer. If we get none, or the wrong one, does it mean that the child doesn't know the name for lamp, or doesn't know what the word 'lamp' refers to? Not necessarily. In other contexts, he might know the word perfectly well. His reason for not answering the question, 'What's that?' may be only that the question itself confuses him, that he doesn't know what we want him to say or do.

Jerome Bruner once said, very aptly, that much of what we do and say in school only makes children feel that they do not know things that, in fact, they knew perfectly well before we began to talk about them. I have often seen this in mathematics, where fifth-graders, confused and frightened by rules and magic recipes, are unable to use either rules or common sense to do problems that they could easily have done a few years before. And what is true of school, is often true of home. A child's understanding of the world is uncertain and tentative. If we question him too much or too sharply, we are more likely to weaken that understanding than strengthen it. His understanding will grow faster if we can make ourselves have faith in it and leave it alone.

One good way to help children learn the names of things is by talking about anything we do together. Many mothers, getting a child ready to go out, say something like this: 'Now we'll tie up this shoe; pull the laces good and tight; now we'll get the boots; let's see, the right boot for the right foot, then the left boot for the left foot; all right, coat next, arms in the sleeves, zip it up nice and tight; now the mittens, left mitten on the left hand, right mitten on the right hand; now comes the hat, on it goes, over your ears . . .' This kind of talk is companionable and fun, and from it the child learns, not just words, but the kinds of phrases and sentences they fit into.

*

One winter morning, when we were eating breakfast, Tommy began to say 'Toe! Toe! Toe!' Putting helpful expressions on our faces, we said, 'Toe?' It was clear that we did not know what he meant. Again he said, 'Toe! Toe! Toe!' looking furiously at us. We knew that he had been using the word to mean toe, coat, cold, and toilet. So we said, pointing at his toe, 'Does your toe hurt?' Wrong. 'Do you want your coat? Your blue coat?' Wrong again. 'Do you want to go towet?' (family expression inherited from previous baby). Still wrong. 'Are you cold?' Now we were on the right track. Asking more questions, we eventually found that someone had left an outside door open, letting in a draught, and that Tommy wanted us to close the door – which we did. This shows that a baby's speech may be more varied than it sounds. He may *know* the difference between a number of words, even if he cannot say the difference.

When a baby shows us, by his expression, by the insistent tone of his voice, and by repeating his words over and over, that he is trying hard to tell us something, we must try just as hard to understand what he is saying. Often it will not be easy. Some people, if they don't understand the first or second time, say, 'I don't know what you're saying,' and give up. But we must not give up. It sometimes helps to ask the next oldest child in the family. He may be able to interpret, perhaps because he knows the smaller child better and hears him talk more, perhaps because he himself is closer to early speech and remembers what it is like. Or, if there is no other child to interpret for us, we can say to the child who is speaking, 'Can you show me?' I remember seeing one mother do this with her little boy. At first he did not understand her question, and looked puzzled. She then took a step or two in one direction, pointing, and saying, 'Is it in here? Is it this way?' Then she went in another direction and asked again, while the child watched, puzzled and intent. After a while he saw what her question meant, and was soon able to lead her to what he wanted to tell her about.

Once, when Tommy was very little, he came to tell me that his teddy bear was stuck between the bars of his crib. Since I couldn't understand him at first, I went through the 'show-me' routine. As soon as he understood me, he led me to the scene of the tragedy. I said, 'Oh, I see. Your poor teddy bear has got stuck in the crib. His head is stuck in the bars. Well, the thing for us to do is to get him unstuck and pull him out. First we have to turn him a little bit, so that his head is pointing the narrow way, and then we just slide him out.' I continued to talk about the bear, and how it feels to be stuck, etc. What was the point of this talk? First, just to make some conversation, and secondly, to show Tommy our ways of saying what he was trying to say, and to assure him that we do have words for talking about such things.

Bruno Bettelheim has many times pointed out that if a child's efforts to get a response from the world and the people around him fail more than a very few times, he may well decide that there is no use in trying. This throws new light on the matter of I.Q. scores. We know that so-called intelligence tests largely measure skill at understanding and using words. We also know that both high and low I.Q. scores tend to run in families. From this it is easy to infer that the kind of verbal skill measured by these tests is inherited from parents. Many educators are beginning to have second thoughts about this; but that this is still part of the folklore of our time is shown by the fact that many biologists are now talking excitedly about the possibility of treating human embryos so as to raise their I.Q. by twenty points. Clearly they still think that the I.Q. measures some inborn ability, rather than acquired skill.

It seems more likely, at least to me, that I.Q. scores tend to run high, or low, in families, because people who are skilful with words are able, most of the time, to encourage the growth of that skill in their children. Such children, when still babies, are encouraged to try to talk by hearing talk around them. When they begin real talking, they are further encouraged, because their parents (and other older people) are persistent and resourceful in trying to understand them. In a family with little verbal skill, a baby can be handicapped, not just because he hears so little talk, but also because, when he does try to talk, he is less often understood, and hence less often encouraged. If people do not try very hard to understand what he says, he may come to feel that most of the time there is not much point in saying anything.

When Patrick, of whom I spoke earlier, was just over two years old, he could not pronounce s, z, sh, ch, or any other sibilant sounds. He just left them out. Words like 'spoon' came out 'poon'. It did not take long to learn to understand him, and when we adults could not tell what he wanted to say, his three-and-a-half-year-old sister could always translate. Nobody fretted about the missing sounds. As a result, the little boy spoke confidently and freely, and before long was able to speak like everyone else. What would have happened if we had dealt with him as we deal with children in school. Instead of giving him time to correct his own speech, to grow competent and confident in making his sibilants, we would have been correcting him every time he spoke. 'No, not "poon", "spoon". S-s-s-s-poon. Say it, spoon, spoon, spoon.' We might have grown more impatient and angry, the child more discouraged and frightened. It would not have been long before he would have become anxious at the very thought of speaking. Perhaps he would have tried to avoid all words with sibilants in them. Perhaps he might have decided to stop talking altogether, since it always got him into so much trouble. Or he might have developed a stutter or stammer; as Wendell Johnson and other speech therapists have pointed out, this is how stutterers and stammerers are made.

Most people who write about the troubles of slum children in school claim that slum children speak badly because their parents do not correct their speech. This leads to two conclusions. The first is that any child whose speech is not continually corrected will grow up speaking like a slum child; the second is that all we need to do to cure the speech problems and defects of slum children is correct their speech often enough. Both ideas are nonsense.

Children can, do, and will learn to speak the language that most people speak around them. If a child grows up where most people do not speak what is called standard English, then we will do only harm if we try to make him think there is something wrong with his speech. It will make much more sense, as some schools are beginning to do, to teach standard English as if it were a foreign language, encouraging a child to talk and write about things that interest him, in the way that is most natural to him, all the time exposing him to as much standard English as possible.

*

I spoke at a P.T.A. meeting recently, and repeated the story of Lisa giving the name 'cows' to a class of animals including cows, horses, and sheep. I explained that we did not correct her because it would be discourteous; because we were too pleased to hear her talk to be worried about 'mistakes'; and because, realizing that she had done some bold and powerful thinking, we did not want to do anything to make her doubt its worth or discourage her from doing more such thinking in the future. I also emphasized that correction was in fact not needed, that the child was soon able, by herself, to get her names and classes straightened out.

A certain number of people are always upset by hearing such stories. Soon after this meeting, I got a pleasant but agitated letter from an intelligent and highly trained psychologist who had heard my talk. How, she demanded, could children possibly learn unless we corrected all their mistakes? Wasn't that our responsibility, our duty? I wrote a long reply, repeating my point and telling still more stories about children correcting their own mistakes. But she seems to be as far from understanding me as ever. It is almost as if she cannot hear what I am saying. This is natural enough. Anyone who makes it his life work to help other people may come to believe that they cannot get along without him, and may not want to hear evidence that they can, all too often, stand on their own feet. Many people seem to have built their lives around the notion that they are in some way indispensable to children, and to question this is to attack the very centre of their being.

Still, even at the risk of upsetting these good people, we must question their assumption, because it is largely not true. Very recently I met Jill, the three-year-old daughter of some friends I had not seen in some time. She was entertaining me in the library, talking away and showing me this or that. At one point she said, 'Do you want to see what my brother teached me?' I said, 'I'd love to.' She stood before me on the rug, put her head down on the floor, leaned over further and further, and finally went over in a somersault. Amazing! 'Now

69

I'm going to do a big one,' she said, and did another. While she was doing several others, I thought about how to fit into our conversation a sentence with the word 'taught' in it. After a decent interval she mentioned her brother again, and I said, 'Does he teach you many things?' 'Oh, yes,' she said. I said, 'You must have been pleased when he taught you that somersault.' 'Yes, I was,' she said. After a few more somersaults, she did something else, and said, 'He taught me this, too.' And our conversation went on.

Some minutes later, when her father was in the room, she showed him the somersault, and then said, 'That's what Jamie teached me.' I was not surprised; it takes time for children to feel confident in a new way of doing or saying something, and to this child 'teached' must have seemed much more reasonable, more grammatically consistent (it is), and more likely to be right than 'taught'. But again, after a decent interval, I dropped another 'taught' sentence into the conversation, and again, next time she had occasion to use the word, she said 'taught'. Nothing more was needed, or is ever needed. Children's senses are keen, they notice everything, and they want to do things like the grown-ups. If we speak well, and they hear us, they will soon speak as we do.

A child who starts to talk is making a very bold leap into the world. Anyone who has learned a foreign language at home, and then used it for the first time in a foreign country, has felt for himself how bold and risky this leap is. Once, while spending a year abroad, I decided to bike from Paris to Rome. Six weeks before starting out I bought some beginning texts and began to study Italian. By the time I reached Italy I had a small vocabulary and some grammar, but I had never spoken a word of Italian to anyone. The day I crossed the border, I rode into a town called Ventimiglia. Being hungry, I decided to buy some bananas. Over and over I rehearsed how I would ask for them: *'Due kilo di banane, per favore.'* It seemed easy enough. I could not see how it could be wrong. But I had a horrible feeling that if I went into a grocery store and said those words, everyone there would roar with laughter. So I grew more and more nervous the closer I came to Ventimiglia, and to the moment when I would actually have to speak. (My fears were groundless – nobody in Italy ever laughed at me, everyone was kind and helpful.) The moment arrived. There was the store. There were the bananas. No excuse to put it off any longer. I summoned up my courage, walked inside, and spoke my piece. The lady behind the counter made a gesture of acknowledgement, cut some bananas off a stalk, weighed them, and gave them to me. I paid, thanked her, and left. My Italian had worked! But this did not make me any the less nervous when the next time came to speak. It took many trials before I began to feel fairly sure that when I spoke my bad Italian to Italians I was at least getting some idea over to them.

A child learning to talk needs the kind of curious, attentive, sympathetic audience that I found in Italy. At first, he is not sure that this language business really works. Even after many years of talking, he may not feel that he can get his most important thoughts and feelings across to other people. There is no time, in all of a child's growing up, when he will not be seriously hurt if he feels that we adults are not interested in what he is trying to say. For most children, this time comes all too soon.

17 July 1961

Lisa (aged two-and-a-half) is usually the first awake in the morning, after me. When she wakes, she begins to talk to herself. It is an odd mixture. Nonsense syllables, funny noises, snatches of songs, remarks about what she did yesterday and may do today all tumble out in profusion. The other day, after talking about something quite different, she paused and then said, 'Going to get dressed, (pause) Dress. (pause) Shoes. (pause) Pants.' Then these thoughts led to something else. She goes on talking all day. Sometimes she talks to get something she wants. Sometimes she talks to make something happen, that

How Children Learn

might uncover the meaning of what she says. Much of the time she talks just because she likes the sound of it.

She likes to talk about colours. One of her favourite words is 'blue'. Something about the action of lips and tongue in the 'bl' pleases her, for she says it often. Whenever she says that she wants something, she usually adds, 'Want a blue one, a pink one,' or 'I have a blue one, a pink one.' She certainly does not know the names of the colours, and may not know, even in the most general sense, what a colour is. What she does know about words like 'blue', yellow', 'pink', and so on, is that they are adjectives. That is, they are combined with other words in a special way. Indeed much of her talk might be called experiments with grammar, that is, exercises in putting together words in the way that people around her put them together. She makes word patterns, sentences, that sound like the sentences she hears. What do they mean? Often they may not mean anything, and are not meant to mean anything. Not long ago she said, in the middle of a conversation about something different, 'I fell out of a big blue mountain into a car.' My mind reeled. What was she trying to say? Then it occurred to me that perhaps she was not trying to say anything, but was making up a nice-sounding sentence, a pattern of words, using words and phrases that she knew and liked to say.

One morning at breakfast she began to say, 'Pass the sugar. Pass the pepper. Pass the toast. Pass the jam.' At first, we passed them along. I noticed after a while that she did not use them. Often she had no use for them; what she asked for had nothing to do with what was on her plate. She would ask for milk when she already had some, or for sugar when there was nothing to put it on. Why was she asking for these things? Clearly, because everyone else was. When you sit down at breakfast you ask people to pass things. The grown-ups were all doing it, so she was going to do it, too.

This may have been one reason for playing the 'please pass' game, but it was not the only reason. I soon saw that, although she did not use any of the things that were passed to her, she watched very carefully each time to *see* what was passed to

72

her. In short, she is using talk to make something happen which will, in time, help her find out what the talk means.

I don't want to make her word-experiment seem more precise than it really was. If she could have put into words her reason for looking carefully at all that was passed to her, I don't think it would have been, for example, 'I'm going to ask them to pass the sugar, and I'm going to watch and see what comes up the table, and then I'll know that's what the sugar is.' It was much more probably something like: 'I'm going to ask them to pass things, and I'm going to watch what they do, and from that I'll probably find out something interesting, maybe what all these things are called.' No doubt she had to ask for, and get, the sugar a good many times before she began, first to suspect, then to feel sure, that the white sandy-looking stuff in the bowl *was* what everyone called 'sugar'. But children are good at gathering and storing this kind of vague information – too vague to be useful to most adults – and waiting patiently until, some day, they find they know what it means. In the same way, a child hearing people say, 'Shut the window,' and 'Shut the door,' and watching to see what happens, will not say, right away, 'Aha! That's the window, and that's the door.' But one day he gets a hunch, and soon he knows. By such means children learn the five thousand or so words they are said to know when they first come to school.

*

One of the wittiest and truest remarks I have ever heard about education was made not long ago by a Catholic educator, a veteran of many years of teaching and teacher training. He was talking to a group of Catholic high school superintendents about handling young teachers, and was urging them not to be too quick to point out and correct mistakes that the teachers, given a little time, might see and correct for themselves. 'A word to the wise,' he said slowly, shaking an emphatic finger, 'is *infuriating*.' We all laughed, because he had fooled us, and because he was so right. Infuriating is just what it is. We all know the kind of person who is quick to interrupt whatever we are saying to correct some unimportant mistake. Strangling seems much too good for him. I blush to think how long it took me to break myself of just that habit.

Most of us are tactful enough with other adults not to point out their errors, but not many of us are ready to extend this courtesy (or any other courtesy, for that matter) to children. Yet it is important that we should, because they are perceptive and sensitive, and very easily hurt, humiliated, and discouraged. For this reason I was careful, when three-year-old Jill said 'teached' to me, to let some time go by before I said 'taught' to her. To have said it right away would have seemed like a correction and a reproof. We should even be careful about mentioning mistakes which they have themselves corrected. They may not like to be reminded of them. Thus, while entertaining me Jill began to sing some of the chorus of 'The Blue-Tail Fly.' As she sang 'Jimmy crack corn, and I don't care', her (very nice) father interrupted her, to say, with pride and delight, that he had never heard her say 'crack' before, that she had always said 'frack'. He spoke only to show his pleasure; in his shoes, I might have done the same. But the little girl, ordinarily not the least shy, became embarrassed and self-conscious, and when she started to sing the song again, could only sing 'frack', and was soon eager to stop singing altogether.

I can think of a comparable experience with Tommy. Once a year, in the city where he lives, they have an annual festival, in which they burn a giant effigy of Zozobra, the King of Gloom. This great bonfire is very exciting for little people to see; for months ahead Tommy was talking about 'Zorzor', and when we were going to see him. The family, when talking to each other, spoke of Zozobra, but when Tommy asked us about Zorzor, it seemed more courteous to use the same word in our reply, which we did. Suddenly, one day, not long before the festival, with no in-between experiments that we knew of, he began to say 'Zozobra'. A day or so later, a member of the family who had not heard him say 'Zozobra' remarked that we would soon see Zorzor. Instantly Tommy said, kindly but very firmly, 'It's not Zorzor, it's Zozobra.'

Perhaps it is for such reasons that most children do not like to hear stories about when they were younger. Infancy is not a blessed state to them, but something to be grown out of and escaped from as quickly as possible. To them, their littleness, helplessness, and clumsiness is not cute, but humiliating, and they want to be reminded of it as little as possible. They don't mind, once in a while, if we don't overdo it, our telling them that they were very nice when they were little, but that is about as much about it as they want to hear. Whatever mistakes they have made, in their growing and learning, are best forgotten.

*

Jill's saying 'teached' instead of 'taught' is an example of the kind of mistakes little children often make in their talk. When we are not thinking of these mistakes as cute, we tend to think of them as ungrammatical, another example of children's unskilfulness in imitating language. The fact is, of course, that a child saying 'teached' is not imitating and is not being ungrammatical. He is inventing, and in a highly grammatical way. He is not saying 'teached' because he heard someone else say it; he probably never did. He is saying it because he knows – though he could not put his knowledge into words – that other verbs form their past tense by adding the suffix *-ed*, and he therefore supposes that the verb 'teach' should behave the same way. This is in every way a reasonable assumption and a first-class piece of thinking. All the more reason why we should meet such 'mistakes', not with a curt correction, but with understanding and courtesy.

*

When I was still teaching fifth grade, I was talking about my class to a twelve-year-old friend of mine. I happened to say that some of the children in my class had been having a conversation. At this my friend looked puzzled. She said, 'You mean these kids were talking about this stuff in class?' 'Yes.' She said, 'Was this in Show and Tell?' I said, 'No, we don't have Show and Tell, but there are lots of times during the day when the kids can talk to each other, if they wish it, about whatever interests them most. Don't you ever have a time in class when you can talk to other people?' She was almost too astonished to answer.

Of course I knew what she would answer even before I asked her. Bill Hull once said to me, 'Who needs the most practice talking in school? Who gets the most?' Exactly. The children need it, the teacher gets it. Even in the most supposedly enlightened schools, the usual rule in almost every class is that a child talks only to the teacher, and then only when called on. In many schools children are forbidden to talk between classes or in the corridors. This leaves only lunch, when they are busy eating, and recess, when they are trying to let off a little steam built up during their long periods of enforced stillness and silence. And I have known more than a few children who have gone to schools where often they were not allowed to talk during lunch, and sometimes even during recess. After school children head for home, where their time is likely to be taken up with homework and TV, and where in any case nobody else may be very interested in talking to them. The result of this kind of education is that children of ten or even older may be no better at talking than they were at five. In fact, I have known many ten-year-olds, in a highly intellectual community, who were nowhere near as good at talking as many five-year-olds I have known.

This loss of skill and interest in talking affects every subject in the standard curriculum. For example, take writing. A child who does not talk will not have many things that he wants to say, and hence will not know what to write about. He will often feel that nothing he might want to say or write could possibly be of any interest to anyone else, and that if he did say or write something, others would only laugh at it. As fast as thoughts come to him, he censors them, rules them out. When he does try to express his thoughts, he finds it hard, because he has had so little practice in putting words together. Because he has never learned in practice what kinds of things make speech clear, forceful, and effective, he will have no way to judge the worth of his own writing. As they say, he will have a tin ear. The test of good writing, after all, is not whether it obeys 'laws of grammar', but what it sounds like. If a student does not know what good talk sounds like, all the rules of grammar in the book will not enable him to write well. And the fact is, as a glimpse at many a learned journal will make plain, that many of our most highly educated men write extraordinarily badly.

Lack of skill in conversation is also likely to make poor readers, at least of many kinds of writing. The good reader enters into an active dialogue with the writer. He converses with him, even argues with him. The bad reader reads passively; the words do not engage his mind; he is like a bored listener at a lecture. Such a reader, studying a text, is very likely to use his mind as if it were a photographic plate, as if by staring hard enough and long enough at words on a page he could fix them in his memory. This never works. In courses like maths or science, in which one must often follow instructions, turn other people's words into action, the inarticulate child often finds that he can't do it. Or he may find that he cannot separate in his mind what he understands from what he does not, or state his confusions clearly enough to enable others to help him. In short, the child in school who is not fluent with words is bound hand and foot. No doubt our schools are too symbol-minded, and should give more time and scope to other forms of expression. Perhaps some day they will. Right now, it is fluency that pays. Yet, in almost all schools, hardly anything is done to help children become fluent, precise, and skilful in speech.

The so-called revolution now going on in education has so far done little to change this. In many classes doing the very latest thing in maths, social studies, or whatever, the pattern of talk is what it always was. The teacher does most of the talking, and now and then asks the children questions, to make sure they have been paying attention and understand. Now and then a bold teacher will start what they call a 'discussion'.

What happens then is usually what Bill Hull calls 'answer pulling'. The teacher asks a series of pointed questions, aimed at getting students to give an answer that he has decided beforehand is right. Teachers' manuals are full of this technique – 'Have a discussion, in which you draw out the following points. . . .' This kind of fake, directed conversation is worse than none at all. Small wonder that children soon get bored and disgusted with it.

Even if class discussions were open, honest, unmanipulated, and genuinely interesting to the young, and even if all children took equal part in them, they would not be enough to give most children skill in speech. There are too many children, and too little time. What is the answer? Simple enough, if we have the courage to try it. In many elementary school classes in England, children are free to work in pairs or small groups, and to talk – if they do it quietly – as they work. In classes where the children are not yet allowed to do independent work of their own choosing, there should be plenty of time set aside for children to talk to each other, about whatever interests them, without guidance or interference from the teacher. There might be times when the teacher would have to ask children to talk more quietly. But he should not control what the children talk about.

In my last fifth-grade class, I used to set aside a period every now and then as a free period. In that time the children could read, or draw, or play games (chess became very popular), or do puzzles, or, as they liked best of all, talk to each other. As time went on, I felt more and more that these periods were perhaps the most useful part of the day. Sometimes the girls' conversations would turn into whispering and giggles, or the boys' into shouting arguments. But on the whole, and more and more as the children gained experience, the conversations seemed to be serious, and very useful to all taking part in them. For one thing, at such times the distinctions between able students and less able broke down. Some of the poorest students were very interesting and well-informed talkers, and could talk and argue as equals with the most successful students in the class. To this, some teachers have said that children who were used to being tightly controlled in class would not know what to do with free time if they had it, and would abuse it. The problem is not as serious as they think, but it is real. One way to deal with it is, at first, to make free periods short, perhaps fifteen minutes or half-an-hour, with the restriction that talk must be quiet. There might even be some periods that could be free but silent. As the children get used to freedom and find interesting ways to use it, they can be given more of it. In such ways we can break out of the school lockstep and make the classroom a place where more and more independent studying, thinking, and talking can go on.

Reading

When Lisa was about three-and-a-half, she was the youngest child of a large family in which everyone loved reading and books. Books were everywhere in the house – on tables, chairs, beds, floors. Yet the family was very relaxed about reading; none of the children had been pushed into it, and nobody was trying to push Lisa. So I was taken aback when one day, out of a clear sky, she said to me, rather aggressively, 'I can read!' I said, surprised, 'Well, sure, I never said you couldn't.' There was no point in challenging her. She knew she couldn't read; she knew I knew she couldn't. Clearly, it was very humiliating to her to know that she could not do something that everyone around her – as far as she knew, the whole world – could do. Why add to her humiliation?

Many years later a friend told me a story about his daughter, not yet a year old. She had been given a little plastic whistle, which she loved to toot. It was her favourite toy. One day one of her parents picked up the whistle, and, seeing that it had holes in it, like a recorder, began to play a little tune on it. They both amused themselves with it for a minute or two, then gave the whistle back to the baby. To their great surprise, she pushed it angrily aside. At the time her father told me the story, she had not blown it since.

The story reminds me of something that Danny once did, when about two-and-a-half. I had thought that he might like the Cuisenaire rods, and I was curious to see what he might do with them. So, one day when I visited his parents, I took a box of rods with me. We opened it and showed him all the little coloured sticks. He was enchanted. Like glass beads to primitive people, these hundreds of pieces of brightly coloured wood looked to him like the most real wealth in the world. We emptied the box out on the rug, and for a while he just sat there, picking up handfuls of the rods and letting them run through his fingers, drunk with excitement and joy, looking for all the world like a proverbial miser with his money. I know now that I should have let him go on playing with the rods in his own way, getting his own kind of pleasure out of them, taking in information about them through his eyes and his fingers, gradually exploring their possibilities. At the time, I felt I had to start him off 'learning' something. So, in what I supposed was my low-pressure way, without even saying, 'Watch', I took some rods from the pile and began to make a pattern of them on the floor, thinking that he would soon imitate me. Danny's father joined me, and before long we had built a simple low structure, that we thought Danny could imitate successfully. When we finished, we looked at him. He looked at us for a while, expressionless. Then, without saying a word, he came over and with one swipe of his hand knocked our little building all over the rug. Amazed, we asked, 'What did you do that for?' He just looked at us. Stupidly, we persisted, and built another structure. Again, he destroyed it, looking not so much angry as determined. We tried once more; same result. Then, at last, we had the wit to see that something was happening that we did not understand, and let the little boy play with the rods in his own way.

It is certain that a child is greatly inspired and helped to learn by what are often called 'competence models' – people who can do things better than he can. But we ought to remind ourselves now and then that sometimes a competence model can be altogether too competent. Child psychologists write a good deal about what they call 'infant omnipotence'. Their theory seems to be that infants and young children really believe they can do anything, and only gradually, as they grow up, learn how little they can do. I do not believe this is true, even of babies; I am sure it is not true even of children as young as two or three, who know all too well how little they know, or understand, or can do, and for whom this awareness is very often frightening and humiliating. This does not mean that we must try to keep our superior knowledge and competence a secret from children; it would be impossible even if it were desirable, which it isn't. But we must be aware that their ignorance and clumsiness are often painful to them, and we must be careful not to rub their noses in their own weaknesses. Parents who do everything well may not always be good examples for their children; sometimes such children feel, since they can never hope to be as good as their parents, that there is no use in even trying.

This is just as true of teachers. One of the reasons why children learn so well from children a little older than themselves may be, not just that the older child understands the language of the younger and can speak in his terms, but that he is a more helpful competence model because he is more within reach. No doubt it is exciting and inspiring for a child interested in athletics, or music, or dancing, or art, or drama, or whatever, to see, once in a while, adults who do those things superbly well. But as day-to-day examples, these experts are probably much less useful to a child than slightly older, slightly bigger children who do things slightly better than he can. I see now, as I may not have at the time, that one reason that many more children at school were interested in blowing on my bugle than on my flute may have been that, for them, I was an expert on the flute, whereas on the bugle I was a rank beginner like themselves.

But let me return to Lisa, who first taught me this, or at least opened my eyes and my mind to it. When she was about four, I made one of my frequent visits to her family. Knowing her interest in reading, I brought with me some materials that I had been using in teaching reading at school – some charts associated with a method called Words In Colour. By this time, I knew better than to try to give these materials the hard sell; children learn very early to be wary of too much adult enthusiasm. So, instead of saying, 'Oh, Lisa, I've brought the most exciting things for you to look at, wait till you see them, we're going to have such fun with them . . .' I merely left the charts

in my room, where I knew she'd see them when she went in
to explore. Sure enough, a few days later, she asked me, 'What
are those big signs in your room?' I said, 'You mean those
things with the coloured letters all over them?' 'Yes.' I said
that they were things I had to use at school with children who
were learning to read. She said, 'Can I use them?' I said, 'Why,
sure, I suppose, if you want to.' She said, 'I mean, right now.'
So we took the charts into the living room, spread a few of
them on the rug, and began to work.

Ordinarily a teacher using these charts points to certain
words and asks children what they are. But I had learned by
this time that even little children can get very frightened,
cautious, and defensive when put into a spot where they have
to give an answer which may be wrong. What I did was to
give Lisa a pointer, and invite her to ask me what any word
said, or, if she felt that she knew what it said, to say it herself. In other words, I was trying to put her out of danger and
in control of the game. For a while, we played this way; she
asked me words, I told them to her, sometimes she knew a
word and would say it herself. But within a very short while,
only a few minutes, she began to change the rules of the game,
to play it in a different way, her way. The older children in
the family had a good friend named Henry Harrison, whom
Lisa knew, and she began to amuse herself by pointing to
various three and four letter words on the chart and saying,
'Henry Harrison!' I tried gently to steer the game back to
where it had been, but no use. It was clear that she was not
only tired of the game, but beginning actively to dislike it. Sure
enough, in another minute or so she said she wanted to stop,
we put the charts away, and for the rest of the visit she did
not ask to see them again.

This was a mystery. Why, when I had been so careful not to
put her on the spot, did she so quickly turn away from these
materials, that she herself had demanded to use? This happened again, with some quite different materials, on a later
visit. Only after some time and much thought, did I begin to
suspect what the trouble had been. No matter how hard I

tried to keep the game unthreatening, to avoid putting her in a spot where she might be wrong, I could not hide the fact that this was a game about which I knew everything and she nothing, and this alone was more threatening and humiliating than she was willing or able to bear.

It would be a great mistake to assume that this is an unusual or peculiar or unhealthy reaction. It is a very human one, as common among adults as children. Most of the time, most of us do not like at all to be confronted with someone who knows a great deal more about something than we do. Though I have recovered a lot of the child's curiosity that I lost during my schooling, I still often sense this reaction in myself. Just the other day, flying back to Boston, I sat next to two men who were having an animated conversation about advanced biology. On the one hand, I couldn't help being curious about what they were saying and the diagrams they were drawing. But even as I tried to catch some shred of meaning from all their talk, in another part of my mind I was angrily rejecting the importance of what they were talking about. I was able, for the most part, to silence my defensive thoughts, and go on listening. But the reaction was there, and strong as it is when I read, say in *Scientific American*, an article of which I can make absolutely no sense. Such reactions are natural, if nothing to be proud of. Even in the privacy of our own minds, we do not like to be made to feel ignorant and stupid. Confronted with what we do not know, we try to protect ourselves by saying that it is not worth knowing.

Proud and sensitive children are particularly likely to react this way. Knowing Lisa to be such a child, I worried a little about what might happen when she got to school and had to submit to formal instruction. Would she resist it? It seemed that she well might. Fortunately she solved the problem by teaching herself to read. Nobody seems to know how she did it. In fact, this is something that, in general, we know very little about. Many thousands of children teach themselves to read, every year; we might do well to find out how many such children there are, and how they taught themselves.

At any rate, Lisa went to a kindergarten where, though the teacher did not try to teach the children to read nor spur them into reading, there were plenty of books, signs, letters, and other useful materials. Finding herself with a crowd of children no more able to read than she was, Lisa must have decided that not knowing how to read was no disgrace. Later, she must have decided that, since older people could read, they must have learned, and if they could learn, so could she. Late in November she began bringing home beginning readers and workbooks, which she worked on by herself. When I saw her again the following summer, she was reading books at about a second-grade, or even an easy third-grade level.

One day she and I were sitting in the living room, both reading. From the children's section of the public library she had just taken out four books, the maximum. Picking the one that looked most interesting, she had settled herself in a big chair and had begun to work on it. I could hear her murmuring, though most of the time I could not hear what she was saying. From the tone of her voice, and her silences, I got a feeling that while there were many words in the book that she knew and could recognize at sight, there were others that she had to stop and figure out, perhaps using her rough knowledge of phonics, perhaps guessing from the context, perhaps both. Some words she was willing to skip; she didn't feel that she had to get every one. But every now and then she would come to a word that she could neither figure out, nor guess, nor skip. On this day she found such a word. Slowly she climbed out of her chair and, holding the book, came towards me. I looked at her as she came. She had a set, stern expression on her face. Pointing to a word in her book, she asked, 'What does it say?' Her look seemed to say very distinctly, 'Now please don't ask me a lot of silly questions, like: "What do you think it says?" or "Have you tried sounding it out?" or anything like that. If I could do those things, I wouldn't be up here asking. Just tell me what the word says; that will be enough.' I told her. She nodded, went back to her chair, and continued reading.

Later I asked her mother how often Lisa asked what a word was. She thought a bit, and said, 'Not very often. Maybe once or twice a week, at most.' Then, as an afterthought, 'It's interesting, though; when she asks a word, she never forgets it.' Interesting, but not surprising; the things we learn because, *for our own reasons*, we really need to know them, we don't forget. But if she only asked other people for words once, or even a few times, a week, this would only account for at most perhaps two hundred of the fifteen hundred or more words that she knew. Where had she learned the others? Clearly, she had figured them out for herself.

*

Another five-year-old, named Nora, taught me more about the things children do when teaching themselves to read, the problems they meet, and the ways they solve or try to solve them. I was visiting her family over a weekend. Though I had not seen Nora since she was a small baby, we were soon friends. Sometime during the day, when I seemed to have nothing to do, she came up to me with a book in her hand and asked if I would help her read it. I said I would, so we sat on the sofa and went to work. The book was *Hop on Pop*, a very good book for beginners. The pictures are interesting and funny, and the words are chosen so as to use very common sounds and words – like those in the title. Also, the book introduces new words in such a way that the child, by using the words he already knows, by looking at the pictures, and by making some intelligent guesses, can figure out almost all the words without help. So it was a useful book for a child trying to teach herself to read.

At first, it was not clear how she wanted me to help her, or what I was supposed to do. Most of the time, I just sat still and silent – a very hard thing for a teacher to do, particularly one who, like me, thinks he is good at explaining and helping. The first few pages were easy; then she began to meet more words that she did not know, and had to figure out. Only rarely, when she seemed badly stuck, did I say anything. Even then I didn't tell her the word, only suggested how she might figure it out. If she had seen it before, I told her so. If she had had words that rhymed with it, sounded like it, I told her that. If the word used entirely new sounds, so that she had to figure it out from the pictures and the general context of the story, I told her that. If she still couldn't get the word, I told her to skip it and go ahead, that perhaps next time she saw it, it would be easier to figure out. Most of the time, she went ahead, but if she asked me to tell her the word, I did.

Before long, an odd thing happened. Nora misread a word that previously she had read correctly. This happened a number of times. I found myself feeling puzzled and annoyed, as I had in my own classroom when children seemed to forget things they had supposedly learned. I thought, 'Has she forgotten that word already? Or is she just being careless, not paying attention, not making an effort?' But this was not it; obviously she was reading the book as well as she could, putting all of her concentration into it. So how could she know a word on one page, and not know it on the next? It seemed almost like stupid behaviour. But she was very bright, and she wasn't bluffing, or guessing, or trying to get me to do the work for her. It was a puzzle.

To understand the learning problems of another person, particularly a child, we must try to see things as if through their eyes. This is often very difficult. It is almost impossible to imagine what it would be like not to know something that, in fact, you do know. Trying to see this book through Nora's eyes, I began to realize that for someone who doesn't know how to read, and who isn't familiar with print, all words must look like funny squiggly shapes, all more or less alike. We think it should be easy for someone to remember what a word looks like from one page to the next. But we *know* the word. For a child, who has only just seen the word for the first time, it is not easy, but hard. It is hard to tell which words on a page are the same, or almost the same, and if they are different, where they are different. We readers have the expert's eye for significant detail; the child does not.

There then popped into my mind an experience I had had some years before, and had completely forgotten. While teaching the fifth grade, I ran across an ad for a British firm that makes type in many oriental languages. I asked them to send me some samples of printing in many of these languages, which they did. I thought the children would be interested in what other alphabets and writing looked like. They were not, but I was, all the more so because even then I was very much interested in the problems of a child beginning to read. One day I took a sheet of printing in some Indian language, and tried to find the words that occurred most often on the page. It was amazingly difficult. At first the page looked like nothing but a jumble of strange shapes. Even when I was concentrating on one short, common word, it took a long time before I could recognize that word at sight and pick it out of the others. Often I would go right by it without noticing it.

In the same way, it takes a child some time to get used to the shapes of letters and words, to the point where he can see at a glance that this word is like that one, and this other word almost like it, and this other word altogether different. So we must give him plenty of time and not be surprised or upset by what looks like slowness, or stupid mistakes. When a child, having looked for a long time at two words on a page, without seeing that they are the same, suddenly exclaims, 'Oh, I see, they are the same!' we must not think that what he has done is trivial. We must realize that the child has made a real and important discovery.

One of the reasons why children from unlettered homes are at such a disadvantage when they start learning to read may be that they lack this familiarity with the shapes of words and letters. This may also be a reason why we should give children time to get used to, and familiar with, the look of letters and words, before beginning any kind of formal instruction. In fact this is a very good reason, among many others, for letting the child himself decide when he wants to start to read.

Not long ago, a teacher was telling me about her work with young, disadvantaged children who could not or did not read.

At one point she said, 'We have plenty of books in the class-room, and they all like to use them. But they don't read them; they just turn over the pages and look at them. How can I get them interested in *reading* them?' I made a suggestion or two that seemed helpful at the time. Only later did I realize that, for children who had hardly ever seen any, this casual looking at books was a sensible and almost certainly a necessary first step to reading. Before these children could begin to think about what particular letters and groups of letters said, they had to get familiar with the look of letters in general, just as a child learning to talk must first become familiar with the sound of talk. Most children, when they start to read, have been look-ing at, and seeing letters for a long time. This is the experience that these less fortunate children have to make up first.

There is another reason, probably more important, why a child may forget on page 6 what he seemed to know on page 5. We are so used to the feeling of knowing what we know, or think we know, that we forget what it is like to learn some-thing new and strange. We tend to divide up the world of facts and ideas into two classes, things we know, and things we don't know, and we assume that any particular fact moves instantly from 'unknown' to 'known'. We forget how unsure we often are of things we have just learned – even things as simple as a name or a phone number. Therefore we can't understand why a child, having said correctly that the HIM on page 5 says 'him', should say that the HIM on page 6 says something else.

What we must understand is that when the child figures out that the HIM on page 5 says 'him', he does not *know* in the sense that we know, he is not certain, that this is so. For reasons he may not be aware of and could certainly not put into words, he has a flash of insight, a hunch, that this word says 'him'. He tries out his hunch, and it works. But because a hunch works this time does not mean to a child that he can rely on it next time. In fact, he may not even get the same hunch next time. Seeing HIM, he may think that it says something else. He has to get the correct hunch many times, and test it, and see it proved right, before he can feel sure of it. Each time he is right, his hunch becomes stronger and surer; but it takes a long time – longer for some children than others – before it becomes what we think of as certain knowledge.

As I pointed out in *How Children Fail*, the children who always forget things in school may not forget so much because their memories are bad, as because they never dare trust their memories. Even when they are right, they still *feel* wrong. They are never willing enough to bet on their hunch that something is so, to turn it into a conviction that it really is so. Working with bad spellers, for example, I have often found that their first hunch about how to spell a word is often correct. But they don't trust that hunch. They think, 'It must be wrong,' and try to find some other spelling of the word, which leads them to write something that *is* wrong, and thus undermines their confidence still further.

Therefore, when Nora made mistakes in reading I resisted the temptation to correct them, or even point them out. It would probably have made her nervous and timid, afraid to try out her hunches, concerned instead to figure out ways to get the answer out of me. Nobody, not even adults, likes to be corrected. We do not have the self-confidence of Sam Johnson, who, asked once by a lady how he happened to mis-spell a word in something he wrote, answered, 'Sheer ignorance, Madam.' Few adults, and fewer children, can take correction in such a spirit; for most of us, it is a heavy and painful blow at our precarious self-esteem.

But I soon found, to my great surprise, that there was a far more important reason for not pointing out Nora's mistakes. Left alone, not hurried, not pressured, not made anxious, she was able to find and correct most of them herself. It was most interesting to note how she did this. When she made a mistake, she rarely noticed it, at first. But, as she read on, I could feel growing in her an uneasy sense that something had gone wrong, that something she had said didn't make sense, didn't fit with other things she was saying. Let us say that on one page she read HIM incorrectly – perhaps as 'Tom'. At first, she might be satisfied with this. But then, on the next page, she would find something that was inconsistent with that first reading. She might find HIM, where it couldn't mean 'Tom'. Or she might find TOM, and read it correctly. Or she might find some other words with the i- or o-sound. At any rate, she would begin to be aware that something on that earlier page had not been quite right. At first she tried to ignore this feeling. She didn't want to go back; she wanted to go ahead and finish the book. But this awareness of something not quite right would not let her alone. It nagged her, like a stone in a shoe. Finally, after fidgeting and squirming, she would turn the page back in an irritated way and try to find what she had done wrong. Most of the time, she was able to find her mistake, and to correct it.

This happened often. Not every time; some mistakes she never became aware of, perhaps because there was nothing in the text immediately following to make her aware of them, perhaps because she was so interested in going ahead that she couldn't be bothered. But most of her mistakes, she caught. Like many or most young children, she had a strong desire to see things fit together, make sense, come out right. And not just that: she had the ability, when things didn't fit, to find out where they had gone wrong, and to put them right.

What we must remember about this ability of children to become aware of mistakes, to find and correct them, is that it takes time to work, and that under pressure and anxiety it does not work at all. But at school we almost never give it the time. When a child at school makes a mistake, say, in reading aloud in a reading group, he gets an instant signal from the environment. Perhaps some of the other children in the group, or class, will giggle, or cover their mouths with their hand, or make a face, or wave their hand in the air – anything to show the teacher that they know more than the unfortunate reader. Perhaps the teacher herself will correct the mistake, or will say, 'Are you sure?' or will ask another student, 'What do you think?' Perhaps, if the teacher is sympathetic and kindly, as many are, she will only smile a sweet, sad smile – which from the point of view of the child is one of the severest punishments the school has to offer, since it shows him that he has hurt and disappointed the person on whose support and approval he has been trained to depend. At any rate, something will happen to tell the child, not only that he goofed, but that everyone around him knows he goofed. Like almost anyone in this situation, he will feel great shame and embarrassment, enough to paralyse his thinking. Even if he is confident enough to keep some presence of mind in the face of this public failure, he will not be given time to seek out, find, and correct his mistake. For teachers not only like right answers, they like them right away. If a child can't correct his mistake immediately, someone else will correct it for him.

The result of this is a great loss. The more a child uses his sense of consistency, of things fitting together and making sense, to find and correct his own mistakes, the more he will feel that his way of using his mind works, and the better he will get at it. He will feel more and more that he *can* figure out for himself, at least much of the time, which answers make sense and which do not. But if, as usually happens, we point out all his mistakes as soon as he makes them, and even worse, correct them for him, his self-checking and self-correcting skill will not develop, but will die out. He will cease to feel that he has it, or ever had it, or ever could have it. He will become like the fifth-graders I knew – many of them 'successful' students – who used to bring me papers and say, 'Is it right?' and when I said, 'What do you think?' look at me as if I was crazy. What did *they* think? What did what *they* thought have to do with what was right? Right was what the teacher said was right, whatever that was. More recently I have heard much older students, also able and successful, say very much the same thing. *They* could not make any judgements about their own work; it was up to the teachers to decide.

*

Many children learn to read like Scout Finch, heroine of Harper Lee's *To Kill a Mockingbird*. She learned by sitting in her father's lap while he read to her aloud, following with her eyes the words as he read them. After a while, she found she knew a lot of them, and from what she knew had enough information or intuition about phonics so that she could start figuring out words for herself. A friend told me just the other day that his younger brother, when about four, had done just this. As he grew more skilful in figuring out what word his father or mother would read next, he began to see if he could say it under his breath, before they got to it. One day his father paused in his reading and heard the little boy reading away softly to himself, before he realized that he was being noticed.

One father I know used to read to his daughter, when she was about three, out of an illustrated Mother Goose. By the time she was four, she knew the book so well that, as soon as he turned to a page, she could recite, also word for word, all the verses there. This must have been a great help to her when she began, as she soon did, to teach herself to read. From this book she could draw on a fund of words that she could already recognize. From these words, in turn, she could begin to get an understanding of phonics – relationships between written letters and spoken sounds – that would help her figure out other words.

It will probably help many children get started in reading if their parents read aloud to them. However, this isn't some kind of magic pill, and if the reading isn't fun for both parent and child, it will do more harm than good. Tommy, at least when I last saw him, had never shown much interest in being read to. Once, on one of our shopping expeditions down town, I bought him a book, which I let him pick out himself in the bookstore. This was very exciting for him. As soon as we got home, he asked me to read the book to him. He would not let me stop until I had read it all, and through the whole reading he sat quietly and absorbed – unusual for him. But he never asked me to read it again, and showed no particular interest when I suggested it. At that particular time in his life, other things interested him more.

Even children who like being read aloud to, like Danny, don't like it when the parents don't like it. One evening, just before his bedtime, he asked his mother to read to him. She took a picture book from a nearby pile, and began, with a sigh

– she was tired. The book was not particularly interesting, and she had read it many times before. She did her best to make it sound interesting, but children are quick to sense our feelings, and Danny soon began to squirm and fidget. Because the reading was no fun for her, it was no fun for him. Soon he said he didn't want to hear any more.

There's nothing wrong with telling a child, if we don't like a book or get tired of reading it, that we don't want to read it. He will enjoy our reading more if we read something that we like, as well as he. As a matter of fact, since we will probably be asked to read aloud any book that we get for a child, we would do well to make sure that we like most of these before we get them.

There's no reason to feel, either, that we must always read aloud to little children from 'easy' books that they can 'understand'. If we are reading something we like, with great expression and pleasure, a child may well like it, at least for a while, even if he doesn't understand all of it. After all, children like hearing adults talk, even though they can't understand much or most of it. Why not reading as well? Once, when teaching first-graders, I decided to try reading aloud to them something more difficult than the very simple stories they were used to. My choice was *The Odyssey for Boys and Girls*, by A. J. Church – a book I loved when small, but which many teachers would feel was much too advanced or difficult for first-graders. This class, however, liked it very much, and on subsequent days asked me to read more of it.

*

Not long ago, the mother of a seven-year-old child who was not yet reading told me that he had asked her, 'Why should I learn to read? I can tell what all my books are about just by looking at the pictures.' Books for little children, beginning readers, have so few words and so many pictures that many children may not be sure where the story is coming from. They may think that it is in the picture, and that in reading we are just telling a story about the picture. When I was little, children's books contained mostly words and very few pictures. We knew that if we wanted to find out the story, we had to learn to read the words. Remembering this, I one day took into a classroom of three-year-olds a book with no pictures in it at all, sat down in a corner, and in a quiet voice began to read it aloud. After a while, some of the children began to notice, and listen. One by one, they came over to see what I was reading. When they looked in the book, and saw no pictures, they were at first surprised. Then, after more watching and listening, quite a number of them would point to a word on the page and ask, 'What does that say?' I would tell them. None of them stayed for long – it wasn't a very interesting book. But they all grasped the vital idea, new to many of them, that in some way those black marks on the page *said* something.

I have recently heard from his mother that Tommy, who a year ago was very little interested in books, reading, or written words, is now very much interested in what those words say. He continually asks her what is written on cans, bottles, cereal boxes. He likes big words even more than little ones, and he finds it mysterious and exciting that the label that said FRUIT COCKTAIL yesterday still says it today – *always* says it. And indeed it is mysterious and exciting that, in writing, we should be able to freeze and preserve for as long as we want such perishable goods as thought and speech.

I remember the first time I discovered that a written word *said* something. The word was LAUNDRY. I was about four, perhaps a bit younger. Young enough so that nobody had yet started to teach me that words said things. We lived in New York City. In our walks through the streets, to the park or elsewhere, we passed many stores, with their signs. Most of these signs said nothing that would help a child know what they were saying; that is, the grocery signs were Gristede's, First National, A & P, the drugstore signs were Rexall's, Liggett's, and so on. But wherever there was a laundry, the sign over it said LAUNDRY. Ten, twenty, a hundred times, I must have seen that sign, and under it, in the window, the shirts and other clean clothing that told me that this was a place where things were washed. Then, one day, I realized that there was a connexion between those letters over the store, and the shirts in the window, and what I knew the store was doing; that those letters over the store told me, and were there to tell me, that this place was a laundry, that they *said* 'laundry'.

That is all I can remember about teaching myself to read.

*

Jean was a very bright, alert, and articulate child, but she did not learn to read in the first grade. Her parents, and we at the school, thought this was odd, because she was so bright. She didn't seem afraid of reading; she hadn't tried to learn and failed; she just hadn't tried. Her parents, being unusually sensible, didn't fuss or worry, and they persuaded the school not to fuss and worry either, but to let Jean stay with her class. At the end of her third-grade year, though as lively, articulate, and curious as ever, she still was not reading. The school and her parents talked it over, and decided to offer her a choice. They pointed out to her that the fourth grade did a great deal of reading, that almost all their learning came from books, and almost all their talking was about books. It would be very hard, and dull, and confusing for her if she did not read. Did she want to go ahead with her class anyway, or would she rather take another year in the third grade, to catch up? Jean thought about this a while, then said that she would like to stay with her class. By the following winter she was reading as well as any of her very bright and able classmates.

Here is a copy of a letter, written by the mother of a boy who is at one of the schools in which children are not required to attend classes, but learn when and what they like, with whatever help from the older people around them they may choose to ask for. The boy, who had been having great difficulty in his conventional school and had not learned to read, went to this school when he was seven. Two years later his mother wrote:

[he] has not, until the last month or so, attended a single class ... yet in taking the Standard Achievement and I.Q. tests we find he is

reading into the tenth grade, doing maths into the ninth grade, working with electronics and in several other areas that are not offered in public schools, even to the high school student . . .

The electronics suggests how this seeming miracle was accomplished. There are no electronics manuals, texts, and instruction books written for young children. To use them, you must be able to read words like 'resistor', 'capacitor', 'potentiometer', and the like. No doubt this boy had to have help at first; but in learning to read the basic terms of electronics he undoubtedly got enough information about letters and sounds to enable him to read any words he met. To work in electronics, you must also know arithmetic, up through the decimals, so he had to learn that, too, along with a good deal about electricity and electric circuits.

Timetables! We act as if children were railroad trains running on a schedule. The railroad man figures that if his train is going to get to Chicago at a certain time, then it must arrive on time at every stop along the route. If it is ten minutes late getting into a station, he begins to worry. In the same way, we say that if children are going to know so much when they go to college, then they have to know this at the end of this grade, and that at the end of that grade. If a child doesn't arrive at one of these intermediate stations when we think he should, we instantly assume that he is going to be late at the finish. But children are not railroad trains. They don't learn at an even rate. They learn in spurts, and the more interested they are in what they are learning, the faster these spurts are likely to be.

This is not to say that all children, left to learn on their own, would find something that interested them as much as electronics interested the boy I just spoke of. It is to say that when they learn in their own way and for their own reasons, children learn so much more rapidly and effectively than we could possibly teach them, that we *can afford to* throw away our curricula and our timetables, and set them free, at least most of the time, to learn on their own.

Nowhere is our obsession with timetables more needless and

foolish than in reading. We make much too much of the difficulties of learning to read. Teachers may say, 'But reading must be difficult, or so many children wouldn't have trouble with it.' I say that it is *because* we assume that it is so difficult that so many children have trouble with it. Our anxieties, our fears, and the ridiculous things we do to 'simplify' what is simple enough already, *cause* most of the trouble.

How great, in fact, is the task of learning to read? What information, what relationships must be learned, in order to do it? What we have to learn are the various ways in which the letters of written English can represent the sounds of spoken English. How many such sounds are there? About 45. How many letters, and combinations of letters, are needed to make these sounds? About 380. Granted, it would be nice if for each sound there were one and only one letter, as in Italian. But 380 letters and letter-groups is nothing to get into a panic over. How many words does the average child know when he comes to first grade? Five *thousand* or more. And a great many of these words have many more than one definition, as a quick look at the dictionary will show, so that the child knows many more than five thousand word meanings. And this is not all. He knows a great many of the enormous number of English idioms that cause such trouble to foreigners. Moreover, he knows most of the grammar of the language, as well. Though he may not know their names, there are hardly any of the constructions of English that he cannot understand, or use in his own speech. And this is just as true of children in countries whose grammar is much more complicated than English, full of case endings, verb endings, genders, agreement, and all kinds of things we don't have to bother with. All over the world, children learn this extraordinary amount of information, most of it by the time they are six, and most of it, as I have described, by themselves, without anything that we could call formal instruction. Compared with this task, the task of learning to read even English is very, very small. To be sure, it can't be done overnight; but it certainly doesn't deserve all the worry and agony that we put into it. All we accomplish, by our worrying, simplifying, and teaching, is to make reading a hundred times harder for children than it need be.

*

When I went to Europe, and began relearning my long-forgotten school French, and learning Italian from scratch, I was much helped by signs. In those days, at least, most European stores, like our laundries, had a sign over them telling what kind of store they were. This made it easy to learn these words by myself. Also helpful were signs like Entrance, Exit, Men, Women, Telephone, No Parking, Emergency Use Only, Bus Stop, Gas, Restaurant, and so on. It occurred to me later that it might help children. She laughed and said, 'The older one would just tear were many such signs around them in the home. I thought of making, on 3 × 5 cards, such signs as Door, Window, Kitchen Sink, Chair, Table, Stairs, Light Switch, and putting them in the right places. I suggested this to a friend who had some small children. She laughed and said, 'The older one would just tear them all off, and the younger one would eat them.' This set me back a bit. But later, when Lisa was four, and again when she was five, I made a number of these signs, and put them around the house. At first, she seemed not particularly interested in them, though she did look at them, and perhaps learned something from them. When she was a bit older, she became quite interested, and wanted to make some herself.

When Tommy was four I decided to make some for him. By this time I had decided that it would in the long run be more useful to him if I wrote more than one word on each sign, thus: This Is A Lamp, Clothes Closet, This Is The Washing Machine. Though it might be harder at first to figure out or remember what each card said, it would give him more data, from which he could figure out such words as 'This', 'A', and so on. He was very enthusiastic about it, watched me make the cards, followed me around when I put them up, and asked me about them. Following the lead of Sylvia Ashton-Warner, I said that I would make a sign that said anything he wanted it to say. He showed himself very much like the older children – about nine or ten is the great age for this – who cover the doors of their rooms with notices warning people to stay out, on penalty of the most horrible punishments, up to and including death. We had put up in the yard a tent for him to play in, and he immediately asked for a sign saying 'Do Not Go In This Tent'. I made it for him, and he put it on.

Then *he* wanted to make signs. I said, 'Fine!' and gave him some cards and a felt-tipped pen. In the back of my mind was a hope that he would start trying to copy some of the words I had written, or would at least use some of the letters I had written. But he didn't see the task that way. As he saw it, you thought of something you wanted to say, and then you made some marks on a card, and then that was what the card said. What marks you used were not important. Most of his were rough Os and Us. He plunged himself into the task, and soon had his signs all over the place, usually next to one of mine.

Here I made a mistake, showing how addicted I can still be to narrow and supposedly efficient ways of learning. I began to feel that Tommy was so interested in making his signs that he was not interested in looking at or copying my 'real' signs. And indeed he wasn't; the task, as he saw it, was to get cards stuck up everywhere with marks on them. So I decided that this activity probably wasn't very useful, that he was too young for it, wasn't learning anything from it. I stopped making any new signs, and put away the cards and felt-tipped pen. After a while, perhaps most foolish of all, I began to take some of his signs down, leaving my own up. I thought, why confuse him, why not just leave up the ones with real letters on them? Only later did it occur to me that it would have been very useful for him to discover, by himself, that my signs were different from his. This might have led him to see – not study, just see – some of the ways in which they were different.

Only later yet did it occur to me that what he had discovered in making his signs was the most important thing he could have discovered – that writing is a way of expressing one's thoughts, a kind of magic, silent speech. What difference did it make that I could not tell from his marks what he was trying to say?

What counted was that he really felt he was saying something. It is this feeling about writing that so many children never get in school, and that makes all their work with both writing and reading seem so dead, artificial, and impersonal. If from the start they could think of writing as a way of saying something, and reading as a way of knowing what others are saying, they would write and read with much more interest and excitement.

I see now that Tommy's first sign-making has the same relationship to writing English as an infant's first babbling has to speaking English. I should have encouraged him to go on babbling in writing. After a while, almost certainly, he would have begun to think about ways to make his writing like other writing. It would also have been easy to show him, tactfully, that many people could read conventional writing, whereas only he could read his own. In time he would have begun to be interested in making a writing that other people could read.

In this, as in so many other things, we do things backwards. We think in terms of getting a skill first, and then finding useful and interesting things to do with it. The sensible way, the best way, is to start with something worth doing, and then, moved by a strong desire to do it, get whatever skills are needed. If we begin by helping children feel that writing and reading are ways of talking to and reaching other people, we will not have to bribe and bully them into acquiring the skills; they will want them for what they can do with them.

*

I know of a number of schools – there may be many more that I don't know of – in which there is nothing whatever of what we think of as formal instruction in reading, yet in which children learn to read just as well as in conventional schools. Classes are large, 40 children per teacher. Nor are the children special; they are of average I.Q. and often come from homes in which little reading is done. How do they learn? Why do they learn? What happens?

In most of these schools incoming five-year-olds, who do not read, are put in classes with six- and seven-year-olds, who do.

This takes care of most of what we call the problem of motivation. Little children want to be able to do what bigger children can do and do. There are many different kinds of materials in the classrooms that children can read, or use to discover how to read. There are books, pictures with self-explaining captions, pictures drawn by children and described by them, stories written and illustrated by children, groups of rhyming words, and the like. In short, a wealth of materials, evidence, which the children can take in and from which they can make discoveries. Also, there are many people from whom they can get advice and help, when and if they want it.

In a number of these classrooms the teachers were making imaginative use of tape recorders. I have described earlier how helpful it is for many children to hear a story read aloud, while they follow the words with their eyes. Teachers with 40 students cannot do this reading themselves. What they had done was dictate on to a tape a number of the books that were in the class. Often I saw three, four, sometimes even six children sitting around a table, listening over headphones to a story being read aloud, while they read or followed the same story in a book in front of them. There is much here that we can borrow, and perhaps add to and improve.

In many elementary-school classrooms children dictate stories, directly or through a tape recorder, to their teacher, who writes out the stories and returns them to their authors. For many children, these stories are much more exciting to read than some old book. By such means many children who had not been at all interested in learning to read have become interested. In some inner city schools, the children, bored with the commercially available readers, which have nothing to do with life as they know it, are writing their own readers.

Until recently we have been somewhat limited in what we could do with tape recorders by the fact that the machines were too difficult for children to operate and too easy for them to damage. Those whirling wheels! All that lovely tape, just aching to be spilled out on the floor! It was more than most teachers dared risk. But now, with the development of cassette-type recorders, we have machines that are so simple to operate that children could easily be taught both to record and play back on them without supervision. This would make it possible for a teacher, perhaps with the help of some children, to record a tape library to go with many of the books in their book library, so that at any time a child who wanted to hear a book read aloud, and read it at the same time, could easily do so. Or, if there were children of different ages in a class, the older ones could often write out stories that the younger ones had dictated.

Sports

We took Tommy to the pool today – our first trip this year. Right away, he had an accident that would have discouraged most infants his age. He was standing on the first and second of the steps leading down into the shallow end of the pool. This was as far as he wanted to go; he had refused my invitation for a 'ride' in the water. Instead, he walked about on the steps, looking at the water, and feeling it with his hands. Suddenly, as he walked around, he stepped off the edge and dropped in over his head. His older sister, watching close by, had him out in a second, coughing and spluttering, but not visibly frightened. After a short time out of the water, to rest and get his breath and courage back, he was in again. Now he asked for the ride he had refused earlier. I took him in my arms and walked about in the water, which came up to his waist and chest. He clung to me tightly, holding on, as babies do, with arms and legs. Once in a while I would duck down in the water far enough so that it came up to his shoulders, but as he did not seem to like it, I did not do it often. At no time did he relax his tight grip of arms and legs, and after a short time, he wanted to go back to the steps. This was all he wanted to do today.

9 June 1965

Today Tommy was much more eager to get into the water and to take his first ride. He clung to me less tightly, and did not mind it, even enjoyed it, when the water came up to his shoulders. After we had done this a while, I thought I might be able to get him to let me hold him without his holding me. I began by gently loosening the grip of his legs. He did not resist, and seemed pleased to have them free in the water as we walked around. Then, holding his body very firmly in my hands, I was gradually able to get him to loosen his arms around my neck, and to hold on to my arms instead. Thus I could tow him around in something like a true swimming position. After a bit of this I urged him to kick his feet, and moved his legs to show him what I meant. He liked this and began to kick – as he does everything else – vigorously. Now and then, for a short time, I could get him to let go of my arms and have his hands free in the water. Once or twice I was even able to get him to paddle.

His progress in exploring this new element of water was not steady and uninterrupted. The courage of little children (and not them alone) rises and falls, like the tide – only the cycles are in minutes, or even seconds. We can see this vividly when we watch infants of two or so, walking with their mothers, or playing in a playground or park.

Not long ago I saw this scene in the Public Garden in Boston. The mothers were chatting on a bench while the children roamed around. For a while they would explore boldly and freely, ignoring their mothers. Then, after a while, they would use up their store of courage and confidence, and run back to their mothers' sides, and cling there for a while, as if to recharge their batteries. After a moment or two of this they were ready for more exploring, and so they went out, then came back, and then ventured out again.

In just this way, this baby in the pool had his times of exploration, and his times of retreat and retrenchment. At times he let me tow him around freely, kicking his feet and paddling his hands. At other times he gripped my arms fiercely, pulled himself towards me, and by his gestures and expression showed me that he wanted to be held in the same tight and enveloping grip with which we had begun. Or he might even ask to go back to the steps, or to be lifted out of the pool altogether. Then, a few minutes later, he would be back in the water and ready for more adventure.

At one time or another I have watched a number of parents trying to teach their very little children to swim. On the whole, they don't get very far, because they are so insensitive to this rise and fall of courage in the child. Is it because they don't notice? Or because they don't care? Perhaps they feel that the child's feelings are unimportant, to be easily overridden by exhortation and encouragement, or even anger and threats. More probably, people who don't care much how a child feels will not notice much how he feels. In any case, such would-be teachers, even when they are not wholly unsuccessful, lose a great deal, since a child who is allowed to return to babyhood for a while when he feels the need of it, to fill up his tank of courage when he feels it run dry, will move ahead into the unknown far faster than we adults could push him.

Of course, Tommy has always been an exceptionally bold and adventurous baby. Very few children, however carefully and respectfully treated, progress as fast as he does. But the principle is always true. If we continually try to force a child to do what he is afraid to do, he will become more timid, and will use his brains and energy, not to explore the unknown, but to find ways to avoid the pressures we put on him. If, however, we are careful not to push a child beyond the limits of his courage, he is almost sure to get braver.

Tommy's sister Lisa, for example, was much more timid than he is. When she first went to a pool, she would not do anything more than sit on the top step and splash her feet, and her expression and manner showed that she thought that even this was a risky business. It was weeks before she was willing to get as much as waist deep, or allow any of us to give her a ride. It was not until the following summer that she would let us tow her around without her holding on tightly with her arms. But we respected her natural timidity and caution. The result was that she wanted, and learned, to combat her fears and overcome them. Now, at the age of six, she is a fearless skiier, going down difficult trails with children twice her age. In the summer she works hard at learning to swim, which she does as well as most of her friends.

10 June 1965

Today there was a rope stretched across the shallow end of the pool, to make an enclosed space for the little children. Tommy was very interested in this rope, and particularly in the two blue-and-white plastic floats that helped hold it up. He seemed not at all interested in going on from where we had left off the day before, in learning to kick and paddle. Instead, he wanted to investigate the rope and the floats. At first, like any adult, I thought this would divert him from learning to swim. But I was wrong, for he soon discovered that with the rope he could support himself in the water without my help, and used the rope to explore further into this new element. When he first grabbed the rope and tested its strength and reliability, I gradually relaxed my grip and gave him less and less support, until, at least as it seemed to him, the rope was doing all the work. Of course, he was largely supported by the buoyancy of his own body and by the small plastic float he was wearing.

At first I stayed very close to him when he was holding the rope. Then, very gradually, as he got used to the idea of my not holding him, I moved farther and farther away, to give him more sense of independence. The feeling of not being held was very exciting to him. It clearly made big demands on his courage, for after holding the rope alone a short while, he would say, 'Hold me.' Then, after a moment of being held, he would say, 'Don't hold me,' and I would let him go again. As time went on he wanted to be held less and less, and even told me, now and then, to go away. At about this time he discovered that the plastic floats on the rope could be slid along it. This became a very exciting game, and for most of the rest of our time in the water he busied himself with pushing the floats from one end of the rope to the other. He also discovered that while holding on to the rope he could let his feet swing underneath it, so that he was in effect floating on his back. He liked this, though getting right side up again was something of a struggle.

There were many other children in the pool, swimming, splashing, leaping about, and jumping in and out. This made another problem for Tommy. Water was being continually sprayed in his face, and now and then a wave would come up over his mouth, and even his nose. I did not fully realize, until I watched him, that one of the most important and subtle skills that a swimmer must develop is a reflex that automatically blocks his mouth and nose whenever the water rises over them. The expert swimmer does this without thinking, and indeed often learns to breathe through the upper part of his mouth even when the lower part is under water. This baby, naturally, had no such skill. He didn't know how to keep water out of his mouth and nose. He did not even understand that this had to be done. Quite the reverse, in fact; when a wave rose up over his face it so startled him that he was very likely to gasp in surprise, and thus take water down all pipes. Then followed much choking, coughing, spluttering, and often a loud burp. Fortunately it was about as easy for him to get the water out as to take it in. He didn't like it when this happened, and almost always needed to be held for a moment afterwards, but he never cried or asked to leave the pool. Now and then he would say indignantly, 'Too much peoples!' To which I could only agree.

A child finds it easier to learn to be aware of when his nose or mouth is under water, and to act accordingly, in a pool that is not too rough. But this pool was small and crowded, and being in dry country, had no overflow gutters to keep the waves down. We had to find ways to deal with the situation. One helpful game turned up quite by accident. I was holding him close when he got a small surprise mouthful of water, which he instantly and instinctively blew out in my face. I made a great event of this – grimaced, coughed, choked, spluttered. He thought this was terribly funny, and quickly did it again, putting his face in the water to get new mouthfuls to spray at me. This game had several uses. He could see that a grown-up could choke, gasp, and cough, and that he was not the only one to whom such things could happen. Also, he could see that getting a mouthful of water need not be an accident or a calamity. Finally, he could feel that *he* was deciding and controlling whether water was going into his mouth, or out. When he had done this a while I thought I could get him to blow bubbles in the water, and did it for him. He showed no interest in imitating me, so I dropped it.

12 June 1965

Today was the most adventurous of all. As soon as we got into the water he asked me to take him for a ride. So I towed him for a while around the shallow end. He did not hold on to me, but kicked and paddled vigorously. I was able to hold him very lightly, and after a while, gave him no support whatever. I said to him, 'You're swimming, you're swimming!' and from his excited expression it was clear that he knew this was so. Finally I took my hands away from him altogether, and held them out of the water, to show him and his mother that he was truly on his own. A few seconds of this at a time was as much adventure as he could stand, so I was careful to give him a little contact and support before he could be worried by not having it.

Later, while he was resting and warming up in the sun, I did some swimming of my own. As I came to the deep end, there he was with his mother, who told me he wanted to jump off the diving board and have me catch him. I said, 'Are you kidding? You're sure he wants to do that?' He insisted, climbed up on the board, walked out to the end, and without a second's hesitation jumped off. I caught him, and towed him over to the ladder at the side of the pool. Back he came for a second try, and a third, and he would have gone on if there had not been a crowd of bigger children waiting for a turn on the board. But this adventure brought on a crisis. Having jumped off the board, he felt that the whole pool was rightfully his. Next time we began to swim, he asked me to give him a ride on the deep side of the rope. As soon as he got over the rope he headed straight for the deep end and began swimming with all his might. I followed along, and when we got to where I could just stand, I turned him back towards the shallow end. He said he wanted to go all the way to the deep end, and turned right around again. I turned him back. He protested, and turned again. Soon his mother, and then the lifeguard, joined me in telling him that he had to stay at the shallow end, that he wasn't big enough or a good enough swimmer to swim at the deep end. For a while he argued, as best he could, but when he realized that we were really not going to let him swim in the whole pool, he began to cry, or rather, to roar, with disappointment, humiliation, and rage. We could not appease him. It must have seemed to him that he had proved himself, had earned the right to use the whole pool, and that in keeping him in the shallow end we were just discriminating against him.

16 June 1965

Bad weather has kept us from the pool for a few days. Today the sun brought us back again. As we drove down in the car, Tommy said to me several times, 'Don't hold me, John. I do it by myself.' He was clearly rehearsing in his mind what he would do when he got to the pool. It seemed to me that this was the kind of mental operation that many experts say children of this age, and indeed considerably older children, cannot do. When we arrived, and had put his plastic bubble on, Tommy went right into the water and without any help or support from me began to swim. The bubble, riding up between his shoulders, kept him in a fairly vertical position, so that he had to work very hard to make forward progress. Only when another child, playing, or jumping into the pool, gave him a surprise faceful of water, did he stop swimming, and look around for help and support. As soon as he had coughed and spluttered out all the water, he was off again. In this way he made three or four trips across the entire shallow end. This used up most of his store of energy and confidence for the day. Most of the rest of the time, he was content to have me tow him around, or to hang on and play with the rope.

18 June 1965

Today he learned for the first time how to deal with water coming up over his face. He began the day's exploration, as he had done several times before, by jumping off the steps into my hands. However, he must have been feeling a bit more timid than usual, for he asked me to hold him, not just in my hands but in my arms. We had not done this for some time. In this way I would take him back to the steps, from which he would jump off into my hands again. After doing this a few times, he felt bolder, and was willing to swim back to the steps, I giving him only token support. This soon became no support at all; as soon as he reached me he would turn around and swim to the steps or the edge of the pool. After some experiments he found that he could turn himself around in the water, and go in whatever direction he wanted. This was also very exciting. Several times he turned himself in a complete circle, just to show he could do it, and for the fun of doing it.

During one of our breaks, I watched a man trying to teach his three small children to swim. He was a perfect example of the kind of parent I have described, who thinks that by superior will and brute force he can make his children learn whatever he wants to teach them. As we arrived at the pool he had his little daughter, about four years old, in his arms, and was moving her about in the water. She did not resist, but she was stiffly motionless, and looked uneasy. After not much more than two or three minutes of this, the father, a young ex-athlete run to fat, decided that she was ready for serious instruction. His plan was to hold her in the water in a swimming position, that is, face down, or belly down, while she paddled and kicked. In its

proper time, not a bad idea, but this was not the time, or anywhere near it. The little girl suddenly found herself snatched
loose of her grip on her father, and suspended helpless over this
new, and still strange and frightening element. She went rigid
in his hands, arched her back, as if to lift herself out of the
water, and struggled to get loose. No use. Her father held her
tightly, and said, in a louder and louder voice, 'Kick your feet!
Move your hands!' The little girl began to scream, partly in
terror and anger, partly in the hope that if she made enough
noise her father would have to stop. For a while he countered
with threatening shouts of his own: 'Rink! Rink! You stop it!
Do you hear! There's nothing to be afraid of! Be quiet!' But
she held the stronger hand. The pool was surrounded by people,
and as her screams got louder and louder, more and more dis-
approving eyes were turned on him, until he gave up, and
furiously lifted her out of the pool. Not long after this he repeated the process with a little boy. Before our short stay at the
pool was over, he had reduced all three of his children to tears
and terror.

The pool was very crowded that day, kids were jumping in
and out, and the seas were running unusually high. For the
first time Tommy began to be able to deal with the problem
of water in his face. Now and then he would breathe or swallow
some down, and have to be held until he got rid of it. But more
and more, he was able to keep his mouth closed, or if water did
get in, to spit it right out again. He was no longer much troubled
by spray flying in his face. He accepted this as part of being
in the water. In this, as in other ways, he showed that he was
beginning to feel that the water was his element, and that he
was at home in it.

*

Here my visit came to an end, and with it my reports on
Tommy's progress. The styrofoam plastic bubble he wears is
buoyant enough to support him with very little effort on his
part. It seemed to me that the next step was to free him of his
dependence on this bubble, so that he could support himself

entirely by his own buoyancy and effort. One way to do this might be to carve little hunks off the bubble so that it would gradually give less and less support. Another way might be to take him in now and then without the bubble, holding him up with hands, or by a belt around his waist, and gradually reduce this support. Perhaps in a year or two he will himself decide that the bubble is babyish, and that he no longer wants or needs it. Whatever method is used, our experience so far makes it clear that when we use a child's natural desire to explore the new and unknown, and to gain some control over it, without trying to force him faster or farther than he feels ready to go, both pupil and teacher have the most fun and make the most progress.

*

In the field of sports we see clearly how much children can learn without anyone teaching them anything. At one elementary school where I taught, we had a rather poor athletic programme, mostly due to lack of space, partly to lack of time. The fourth, fifth, and sixth grades had a half-hour recess period in the morning, and an hour sports period in the afternoon. Only in the afternoon could we play softball, and then we had to play in a paved yard that was big enough to hold an infield, but not much more. After two years that yard was lost to softball; part of it was fenced in for smaller kids to play in, and much of the rest was turned into a parking lot. Also, the afternoon sports period was cut down to a half hour, and we were moved into another yard a good deal smaller than a tennis court. In most of such practice as we had, I, or David Hardy, the sixth-grade teacher, would rap out balls for infield practice, or occasionally pitch for batting practice. Fourth, fifth, and sixth-graders would do the fielding; third-graders, sometimes even second-graders, would run the bases.

With such limited time and space for practice, we did not expect to get much of a softball team, all the more so as the boys in the school were not outstandingly athletic to begin with. Yet, year after year, we were able to field a competent softball team that could hold its own against other boys of the same age. How did these kids manage to learn this very complicated game? David and I certainly didn't teach them. There was no time, or room, for anything that could be called instruction. No, they learned by watching each other, and imitating. Year after year we would see the same thing happen. Here would be a boy in the third or fourth grade who seemed so hopelessly clumsy, unathletic, and ignorant of all the rules and skills of baseball that it looked as if he could never learn to play. Two years later that same boy would be a competent and often an expert player – and many of them did almost all their playing at school. They learned, as I say, by watching the older boys who did it best, and trying to do what they did.

As a matter of fact, they learned, on the whole, much better than the boys at another school, at which I taught, where there was far more play space, more time given to sports, and where teachers tried to teach softball. The boys in this school spent a good deal of their sports time standing around watching while someone 'explained' something to them. I was then still under the spell of the idea that if you are determined enough you can teach anybody anything. I remember a couple of boys that I was trying to teach to bat and throw. I can still see their sullen but resigned faces, feel their limp, uncooperating muscles, practically hear their thoughts. Here was school brought right out into the play-yard, where they were supposed to be having fun, or at least a moment's respite from school. Small wonder we did not get far. If, instead, they had had a chance to play with, and see, and imitate bigger boys, how much better things might have gone.

Art, Maths and Other Things

One morning, in the first-grade classroom, two little girls, very close friends, got big pieces of paper, and pencils, sat down at a table, and got ready to draw. After some thought, one began to draw a very large tree. She started at the bottom of the page and drew two lines, which came together for a while and then went parallel up the page, almost to the very top before they began to spread out again. Then she made a fork in this trunk, near the top. From the two main branches so obtained she drew several smaller branches, which she began to cover with leaves. All the while, the other little girl watched, and did nothing. After a while I said to her, 'What are you going to draw?' I was not insistent, only curious. She said, 'I don't know what to draw.' I said, 'Why not draw another tree?' She said, without any hesitation or shame, 'I don't know how.'

It was a surprise and revelation to me. Though I like to look at much drawing and painting, I know very little about it. There was almost no art in my own schooling. I can only remember one art class, and one picture that I tried to paint – an owl sitting on a limb of a dead tree, with a full moon behind it; for me, a rather ambitious work. I never finished it. As a result of my inexperience, I had the naïve idea that artists just look at what is in front of them and copy it, getting better at this as they go along. Only recently have I learned that life does not copy itself on paper, and that to make, with lines and colours, an image that looks like something real, takes technique. There is a trick, or many tricks, that have to be learned, practised, and perfected.

Still, it hadn't occurred to me to think of this in children's terms, as children would see it. I thought that at their more primitive level, art was just a kind of copying. So when this child told me that she did not know how to draw a tree, I was startled. It was on the tip of my tongue to say, 'Well, just look at one.' But I thought again. I remembered reading once that many primitive people cannot recognize either drawings or photographs of even the most familiar objects and surroundings. We say, we believe, that a picture looks like life, but it really doesn't. Pictures are flat; life has depth. The business of turning real objects into flat pictures is a convention, like language, and like language, it must be learned.

A picture of a tree, I realized, has somewhat the same relation to a real tree that a map of a town has to the town. The map is like the town, in many ways; but in making a map we put some things in and leave others out. The same with a picture. This little girl, looking at the complicated piece of reality we call tree, with all its colours, shapes, textures, masses, light and shade, did not know which of these qualities to represent with her pencil, nor how to do it.

Two or three days later, I saw the same girls, sitting at a table again with big pieces of paper before them. But this time there was the familiar tree on both pieces of paper, the roots coming in to make the trunk, the trunk going almost to the top of the page, the two forked branches, the smaller branches sticking out any way, the green leaves. I said, 'Ah, I see you're drawing a tree.' She gave me a pleased smile, and then, nodding towards her friend, said, 'She showed me how.' And then went on with her work.

In the same class was another girl who loved to draw as much as any child of that age I have ever known. She worked hard and quickly, and turned out picture after picture. The walls of the room were covered with them. All of them were interesting, both to me and the other children. She always drew more or less the same thing – a house, with people in and around it. But she varied the drawings in many ways, in the shape of the house, in the kind of garden and trees that grew around it, in the people and the things they were doing.

These pictures were large and full of life and activity. What was most remarkable about them was the extraordinary amount of detail she put into them. When she put grass around a house, she didn't just make some slashes of green crayon; she drew blades of grass, and coloured them. When she drew flowers, she put on leaves and petals. Her people always had five fingers on each hand, and in the right proportions; and on each finger she put a correctly shaped fingernail. After a while she began to put curtains inside the windows of her houses, carefully pulled aside, like the curtains in a real house.

Some of the people who have made a fad or cult of psycho-analysing children's art might at this point make learned noises about this child's obsession with detail, compulsive character, etc. There might be a tiny fragment of truth in this, but no more than that. This was a very gay and energetic little girl, one of the leaders in her class. She drew as she did because she liked to look at things and draw them the way she saw them. Art was her way of expressing much of what she was learning about life. It sharpened her eyes as well, and gave her an idea of what next to look for. And not only her eyes, but the eyes of many of her classmates. A number of them, without think-ing of it this way, made themselves into a kind of school under her leadership, like the schools of the old Italian masters. They drew pictures like hers, or used her ideas and developed them in their own ways. The kind of carefully and surely observed detail that she put in her pictures began to appear in others' work as well. Children would go up – I used to hear them – and look at one of her drawings, and notice that the people had fingernails. 'Look!' they would say. 'They even have fingernails.' It seemed a wonderful achievement. Then they would think of putting some fingernails on the people in their own pictures, and they would look with a new eye at their own fingernails, to see what they really looked like, how they were shaped, how big they were. Or they would begin to try to find some details that his little girl, their leader, had not yet thought to put in.

I wish I could report that this tremendously productive and self-renewing process continued and grew throughout the year. It didn't. This was not because of the teacher, who was a very understanding and gentle woman, and gave these children much more time for art than would most first-grade teachers. But she was under the pressure of the curriculum, the academic lock-step, and both she and the children were under the pressure of the nervous parents, worried about their children's 'progress' – that is, whether the Ivy League express was running on schedule. The children began to feel, after a while, that there was no time for art, that it was not serious – and six-year-olds in school are very serious. They are also very sensitive to what adults value. They show a parent or teacher a picture, and the adult says, in a perfunctory voice, 'How nice, dear.' Then they take home some idiot work-book, whose blanks they have dutifully filled in, and their parents show real joy and excitement. Soon the pictures get shoved aside by the work-books, even though there is more real learning in a good picture than in twenty work-books. When, in later years, the children do draw pictures, they are very likely to draw them more as an escape from real life, like the war scenes of third-grade boys, or the horses that ten-year-old girls interminably draw, than as a way of getting in touch with real life. Not that art as a way of expressing fantasy, fears, and hopeless wishes hasn't value. But this kind of drawing is liable to be furtive and trivial, done on the edges of note-books and homework papers. It is no longer bold and serious.

When I was very young, hardly more than six, if that, my father brought to our apartment, one day, a friend who was an artist. After a while he took out a big drawing pad and a soft pencil and began to draw. Before my fascinated and unbelieving eyes, there began to appear on the paper – a knight! In full armour! It was a miracle. One minute, blank paper; then, a line here, a line there, the hand working smoothly and surely; and there he was, almost as real as life. I would not have been much surprised if he had stepped right off the page. Certainly there was nothing that I wanted, then and for some time, as much as to have been able to do what that man did – put life on a page with a pencil. It seemed a superhuman skill; I couldn't imagine being able to, but I would have given anything to have been able to do it myself.

It is hard to imagine a child in school today having such an experience. It is good that they are allowed and encouraged to paint big, sloppy, colourful pictures with poster paint, without anyone leaning over their shoulder telling them to do it this way or that way, or that what they have done is wrong. But there are possibilities in art that they can hardly have dreamed of, as I would never have dreamed of anyone being able to make that knight. They ought to be able to see more of those possibilities. They should at least be exposed to the idea that art can be, not just a diversion, but a very powerful way of getting in touch with and expressing reality. In short, they should meet some people who can make real things appear on paper. No doubt many children would not choose to explore reality in that particular way; they would rather do their exploring through books, or construction, or machines, or experiments in any one of a number of sciences. But some children would choose the way of art, like the girl in the first-grade class, and their serious work would be a great benefit to themselves and many children around them.

Art can exercise the brain, as well as the eye and hand. I said in *How Children Fail* that the test of intelligence was not how much we know how to do, but how we behave when we don't know what to do. Similarly, any situation, any activity, that puts before us real problems, that we have to solve for ourselves, problems for which there are no answers in any book, sharpens our intelligence. The arts, like the crafts and the skilled trades, are full of such problems, which is why our skilled artists, artisans, and craftsmen are very likely to be sharp-witted people. Their minds are active and inventive; they have to be.

An example of this came up not long ago. A friend of mine, when a grown man, started to paint. When he had been at it a year or two, I asked how it was going. He said, fine, but there was one problem he couldn't seem to lick – he couldn't get water to lie down. Seeing my blank face, he explained. He liked to paint landscapes, and was getting fairly good at them; but every time he tried to paint a lake or pond, his water didn't look like water at all; it looked like a sheet of blue or green or grey glass sticking straight up out of the ground. He showed me a couple of pictures, and it was so. We parted, but I couldn't get his problem out of my mind. I kept asking myself, what is it that, seen by the eye, tells our brain that what is in front of us is a horizon surface of water and not a vertical sheet of glass. What are the cues and clues?

One day, walking down by the Charles River, I began to look carefully, to see if I could find an answer to the question. Of course, there are many. If there are waves, they seem bigger close up; at a distance they lose their individual identity and fade into a rough texture. If there are things along the bank, they get smaller as the bank gets farther away; in other words, perspective tells us that the edges of the body of water are not all the same distance from us. If the water is calm, things are reflected in it. Even where perspective gives us no sure sign that some parts of the body of water are farther from us than others, colour change would do it – things farther away are fuzzier, more blue and grey. For some reason, finding the answer to this question gave me great satisfaction. I had solved a mystery, and saw, and thought, a little more clearly than before.

Because I am ignorant and unskilled in drawing and painting, I could not give many ideas or much inspiration to the children I worked with. But I was able to do a couple of small things that aroused their curiosity and interest, and these possibilities for learning and growth stretched out into the future. After teaching fifth grade for four years, I spent a year as a kind of roaming teacher, developing ideas and materials, most but not all connected with teaching maths. Most of the materials I wanted to use I had to make myself. Usually my raw material was the cardboard that laundries put in shirts. It was cheap and easy to work with. Some of the time, I worked in my own office-classroom, but as time went on I did a good deal of my manufacturing in other classrooms, the teachers permitting, where children could see what I was doing, and, if so inclined, wonder about it, and perhaps imitate it.

One day I was in a first-grade classroom, and for the first time in that room, began to make some small, open-topped cardboard boxes, of just such dimensions that various sizes of Cuisenaire rods would fit neatly into them. I had a drawing board, a T-square and triangles, a ruler, and a sharp knife to cut the cardboard. All this material was interesting to the children. Every now and then, in the midst of their normal class business, they would come over to the corner where I was working, and watch me for a second or two before leaving. Sometimes they would ask what I was doing, to which I would reply, 'Oh, just making something.'

By the time I had finished a few boxes they could see what my work was all about. They wanted to make some of their own. So, when there was time in their schedule, the teacher gave them pieces of a heavy paper known as oak tag, and some scissors, and told them to go ahead. Off they went. By watching me, or each other, or by thinking, or by trial and error, they all figured out that to make a rectangular box with an open top you had to cut out a piece in the shape of a heavy cross. At first these shapes were very crude, the sides not carefully measured, if at all, and the corners not square. But children have a great deal of what might be called a sense of workmanship. When they are not bribed or bullied, they want to do whatever they are doing better than they did it before. So they began to make their boxes more carefully, trying to figure out how to cut them so that the sides would join evenly along the edges, and so that the top of the box would be smooth. Nobody asked me for advice. Now and then someone would watch me doing it for a while, and that was all. Then they went back to work.

I watched their work for a bit – not as long as I would have liked, I had other classes to work with, and some special classes to teach, and a number of kids to 'tutor', which meant cramming them in the hope they could pass some kind of test. So I didn't have as much time as I would have liked for leisurely exploration, or to pursue a promising lead. And the first-grade teacher, naturally, felt she had to get through her curriculum, and get those children ready for second grade. So they were not able to spend enough time making boxes to explore and develop some of the mathematical possibilities that lie in such work – making boxes of exact dimensions, making boxes to hold certain quantities of wooden cubes, making boxes of shapes other than rectangular, and so on.

However, in the short time that they were working on them, one little boy did a remarkable piece of work which in time might have led him and the class in directions I had never even thought of. Incidentally, he had been one of the more troublesome members of quite a troublesome class. After making a few boxes with open tops, he began to think about the problem of making a box with a closed top. He soon figured out what shape piece he had to cut out in order to do this. Then, looking at his closed box, he began to think of it as a house, and drew a door and some windows on it. But this wasn't a very interesting, or house-like looking house. He began to think how he might make a house that really looked like a house, with a peaked roof. I didn't see him work on the problem, and don't know by what steps he managed it, but within a few days his teacher showed me a cardboard house, with peaked roof, that he had cut out in one piece. It was well made, too; the sides and the roof fit together quite well. And he had cut out, not drawn, the doors and windows, before folding the house together. A most extraordinary piece of work.

In such work are many possibilities for further exploration and learning. This particular child, and class, had no time to explore them. But in a different kind of class and school, they might have gone on to do quite a number of things. We can imagine them making models of many differently shaped objects; or making models of one object, but in various sizes, the shape remaining the same but the scale changing. Children are very interested, indeed fascinated by the idea of scale. That things can be made the same shape, that is, to look the same, but some of them bigger than others, is a great mystery and wonder to them. One teacher I knew made, for demonstration purposes, a giant set of Cuisenaire rods, which her children loved to look at and work with. With this somewhat in mind, I made, of cardboard, a miniature set of Cuisenaire rods, to about two fifths the scale of the real ones. A number of first-grade children were much taken with them. They were amazed and delighted to see that relations that held true for the real rods, also held true for these miniature ones.

There are also great possibilities in scale drawings. I remember when I was little seeing somebody make a big copy of a small picture by putting the small picture on a grid – squared or graph paper – and then transferring it to a bigger grid. I think I even did it once or twice myself, and was always amazed to see that it worked. But this was not part of our regular schoolwork; if we did such things, we had to do them at home, or if we did them in school, we had to be careful that nobody saw us. I can easily imagine, however, that a class of young children, starting with a small line drawing, could be fascinated with the idea of making that drawing bigger and bigger, until they had a copy big enough to cover a large part of a wall or a chalkboard. This, in turn, could easily lead into the idea of coordinate points, graphs, and analytic geometry, representing pictures by things that were not pictures, but functions. Or, in another direction, it could lead to the idea of making accurate drawings, to various scales, of real objects, and from there to measurement, not only of lengths but of angles, and to map-making.

It is easy to see how much arithmetic there would be in this. One of the fundamental ideas behind most of what we do in school is that children should and must spend many years memorizing a lot of dull facts before they can begin to do interesting things with them. This is a foolish way to go about things, and it doesn't work. Most children get so fed up with learning the dull facts that they quit before they get enough of them to do, or even to want to do, anything interesting with them. And even of the children who do learn all the facts, most have their wits so dulled in the process that they can't think of anything interesting to do with them, but just go on accumulating more and more – which accounts for too much of the activity in our graduate schools and universities. But if we get the horse in front of the cart where it belongs, if we get children to do things that require them to find and make use of otherwise dull and useless facts, they learn these facts very rapidly – like the boy I described who, as a result of working on electronics, gained nine years of skill in reading and maths in two years, and without ever going to a formal class.

Another time, I introduced the first grade to the idea of isometric drawings. It is easier to show what they are than to say. Suppose I have a cube in front of me. An isometric drawing of that cube would show three faces of that cube, the top and two sides, and would be so drawn that all the edges were the same length. The vertical edges of the cube would be shown by vertical lines on the paper; the horizontal edges, by lines going to right and left at sixty degrees to the vertical.

Isometric drawings are used by draughtsmen to give three-dimensional views of objects. There is a kind of paper called isometric paper, on which are ruled vertical lines, and lines going up to the right and left at sixty degrees to the vertical. With a ditto machine I made some of this paper, and took it down to the first graders. At first I used it to make coloured patterns, using pastel crayons or coloured magic marker. Some interesting shapes and patterns came out, and it wasn't long before the children were asking me if they could have a piece of paper so that they could do some of this themselves. Which they did.

One day, while I was in a first-grade class, half visiting and watching, and half working on my own work, the idea came of making an isometric drawing of a house with pitched roof and dormer windows. This raises some interesting problems, as anyone will find out who tries it. The main part of the house was easy to draw, as were the doors and windows, and the roof was quite easy. But when I began to try to figure out how to make the dormer windows fit into the roof, things became more difficult. Here again, as I puzzled and worked on this, children began to drift over now and then for a few seconds, to see what I was doing. After a while, some of them wanted to try to make some isometric drawings. First they drew simple boxes; then they began to draw flat-roofed houses, with doors and windows. Sometimes, drawing their windows, they would forget that a line that in life was horizontal, had to go up at sixty degrees to the vertical in the drawing; but when they had made this mistake, they would almost always notice, after a while, that it looked funny and wrong, or someone would point it out to them. Then they would come over to take another look at mine, to see how I dealt with the problem. Some of them even began to grapple with the problems of drawing a pitched roof – which for a first-grader is hard. Again, we had little time to pursue this activity, but it was clear that the children were very interested in it, and might have learned a lot from it. Like the work we did with boxes, it stretches out in several directions. We can imagine children making isometric drawings, to various scales, of a number of real objects; or exploring the relations between conventional scale drawings, which show front-view (or elevation), side-view, and top-view; or going from one kind of drawing to the other. And still more interesting problems and possibilities would arise if we introduced the idea of perspective. Little children, like primitive painters, do not get much depth into their drawings, because, like the little girl with the tree, they don't know how, and have never even considered the problem. Suppose they were challenged with this? We could hardly expect little children to discover the idea of perspective for themselves, though here as in other places they might surprise us; but they could certainly see for themselves the need for it, and would be delighted to see that there was a way of drawing railroad tracks that looked the way railroad tracks really do look.

I said earlier that art, in this very strict sense of representing the appearance of things on paper, exercises the mind as well as the eye. Once I asked my fifth-grade class to draw me a picture of a bicycle. Instantly thumbs went down on the panic button. What kind of bicycle? The kind you ride, the kind that you see out in the school yard, a regular two-wheeled bicycle. Boy's or girl's? I don't care. So they began to draw. There was no question here of prior skill; only one or two of the children in the class really liked to draw for pleasure – this after years of school 'art', in schools that believed, or said they believed, that art was important. And even they didn't like to draw bicycles. After some time, except for one or two deliberate failers who refused even to try, the children gave me their pictures. They were extraordinarily revealing. The kids in the class who were intelligent, whose minds were still active, who were still interested in how things were instead of right answers and staying out of trouble, drew bicycles that looked more or less like bicycles. They may have been wrong in detail, here and there, but their bicycles made some sense. Clearly, they had thought, as they drew, about how a bicycle is made and works. They had all drawn some kind of frame; the wheels were attached to the frame; there was some way of making the wheels go round. But the other children, the defeated, drew the most extraordinary collection of shapes. They had very little connexion with a real bike, or for that matter, with each other. I could usually make out what were supposed to be wheels, but they were rarely connected to anything else at all. Two or three vague parts of a bicycle floating in the air, is what most of them looked like. So I took a number of these children outside, with pads and pencils, and sat them down in front of a bicycle, and asked them to try again. The results were hardly any better. With the bike right before them, they could not see how it was put together, or if they could, could not hold that knowledge in mind long enough to transfer it to paper. It seemed as if their schooling had been for so long so far removed from reality that they were no longer able to see reality, to grasp it, to come to grips with it.

If children could do more of the kind of work I have described and suggested, they would get, not just knowledge, but skill. This is important to a child. To be able to do something well, to get visible results, gives him a sense of his own being and worth which he can never get from regular schoolwork, from teacher-pleasing, no matter how good he is at it. There is too little opportunity for this in school. In my own high-priced and high-powered education, there was virtually none; until I was about thirty, the only things I ever *made* were some model aeroplanes, and those out of school, and only when I was nine and ten. This was, and is, a mistake. Maria Montessori showed, among other things, that children could make, and like to make, movements that are careful and precise, as well as movements that are exuberant. Some of the time, at least, children like to be careful, when it is the work or the situation, and not some grown-up, that demands it. We should give them many more opportunities and ways to use and develop skill and precision.

*

An afterthought. I hope no one will mistake me as saying that we should scrap our present curriculum, then make a new curriculum out of what I have been talking about, and put it in place of the old one. I am only suggesting some of the things that children might like to see done in school, and might like to do themselves, were they free to choose. But they must be free to choose whether to explore the world in this way, or any one of a number of other ways. If we merely substitute *Isometric Drawing I* or *Model Building I* for *Arithmetic I*, with the same old business of assignments, homework, drill, and tests, we will have gained little, and probably nothing.

*

During the year that I was doing the work just described I took over one of the first-grade classes for a week while the teacher was out. It had been her custom each morning to put some arithmetic problems on the board for children to see when they came in – problems which they could do while waiting for the organized day to begin. These were usually problems in addition. There were rarely more than two numbers to add, and the sum was rarely over 10, never over 20, because the children had not learned – i.e. been told – how to do such problems.

One day there was a happy accident. I had forgotten to put

the problems up. Two or three children came in early, saw no problems, worried for a while, and then asked if they could put some problems up. (All little children, and some maybe not so little, like to write on the blackboard.) I told them, sure, go ahead. They began by writing some of the kind of problems that had been up there. But after a while they grew bolder, and began to write problems like $70 + 20 = $? Quite often they would get into an argument among themselves as to what was the right answer. They were never willing to leave a problem unless they felt they knew how to do it. Usually they would manage, within a short while, to come to an agreement, and usually the answer they agreed on was correct. It is hard to get honest agreement on any answer that is not correct. Only rarely did they appeal to me, and then only when they got into an argument in which a number of them were all sure they were right. After a while they began adding things like $200 + 400$, or even $230 + 500$, or $340 + 420$. Step by step, making their problems more complicated all the time, the children – not all of them, but a good many – worked out for themselves most of the rules for doing addition. In a week – working only a few minutes a day – they covered material that the school was prepared to spend years teaching them.

At the end of the week, just as they were beginning to get going, I had to leave, and so wasn't able to give their work the kind of nudge that might have led them to consider the problems of carrying, or of subtraction. But I saw enough to make me feel that if arithmetic were treated as in fact what it is – a territory to be explored, not a list of facts to be learned – children, at least many children, would move into it faster than we would have dreamed possible.

Thus, in the prospectus of the Green Valley School (Orange City, Florida) George von Hilsheimer, who founded this and other schools and institutions based on human freedom, writes:

Students who begin at this school have no fear of maths. We have had the pleasure of seeing five-year-olds doing maths for their bedtime 'story' and complete the Work-books for Kindergarten, First, Second and Third Grades *in four nights*. We cannot offer the hope of this progress to summer students, nor to regular students entering after the first grade.

*

One day, this same year, I found myself thinking of the boy in fifth grade who had told me that between 100 and 200 there were 164 whole numbers. I had felt, intuitively, that children felt that numbers grew more dense, so to speak, as they grew bigger; in short, that there were more whole numbers between 900 and 1,000 than between 100 and 200. Even if they had some common sense about small numbers, this began to leave them when the numbers got big enough – as may well be true of all of us – and their heads began to swim, and their guesses grew wilder and wilder.

I thought first- and second-graders might be interested to see how numbers grow, and also to get a concrete idea about the size of certain numbers. One day I bought one of the rolls of paper that go into an adding machine, brought it into the first-grade classroom, and without a word to anyone, began to measure off dots on the roll, two inches apart. When I had a number of these I began to label them – 1, 2, 3, 4, 5 – a number over each dot. Before long, as always happened, someone came over to look. They asked what I was doing. I told them to watch. They watched for a while, then went away; others took their place. Now and then a child would say, 'What's that for?' It seemed to me that the question meant, 'Are we going to have to do something about this?' and I usually didn't answer. If a child asked point blank whether he was going to have to make one, I said, 'Goodness, no!' As this went on, the numbers grew. The word got around as I neared 100, and children came around to watch me write it. It was like the magic moment when a whole lot of 9s on the car's hodometer (the thing that tells you how many miles you have gone) turn into 0s.

Eventually someone said, 'Where did you get the paper?' I named the store. 'How much did it cost?' 'Twenty-five cents.' 'Can I have one?' I said, 'Sure, if you'll pay for it.' I thought this would be the end of it. Not at all; next day a couple of

the children showed up with a quarter for their own rolls. I
bought them, and they went to work. Before long there were
more than a dozen first- and second-graders working on their
own number rolls. Some of them just wrote out the numbers,
not spacing them carefully; others copied me in making
the numbers a uniform distance apart. The numbers grew
and grew. Many children continued up into the hundreds.
I kept working on my roll – eventually I had to splice a new
roll to the old – until it reached 1,500 or so. But two boys, both
interested in numbers and competitive to boot, took their rolls
home to work on, and before long had passed me, getting close
to 2,000.

People may say, did say, in fact, 'What good is all this? What
are the children learning?' Meaning, of course, what questions
can they answer, what tests can they pass, as a result of what
they were doing? I am not sure what the children learned.
Different ones probably learned different things. I suspect they
learned something about the rate at which numbers grow, and
about the meaning, in concrete terms, of some of the numbers
they had been working with in arithmetic. One day, when my
tape had become fairly long, up to about 500 or so, we
unrolled it to its full length. We had to go around the room and
then out in the hall to get to the end. Children walked curiously
and eagerly up and down the length of the tape, saying, 'Here's
200,' 'Here's 400,' and things like that.

I had many plans for continuing this the following year, but
the money that was supporting this work – a few thousand
dollars a year – ran out, and I had to stop. Not without a certain bitterness, when I thought of the kind of money that was
being spent in education, and the things for which much of it
was being spent. It seemed that number rolls could be used in
a great many ways, leading into multiplication, factors, large
numbers, proportion, scale, measurement, map-making – who
knows what?

But the matter of freedom, to choose how to do this, or to
choose not to do it, is all important. Long before the 'New
Maths' had ever been heard of, before the great boom in curricu-

lum reform was under way, Bill Hull was trying to get his fifth-grade classes to do some real, original, problem-directed thinking. One piece of equipment he used was a balance-beam, a piece of wood balanced at its midpoint, with places along the arms to put weights. The children were supposed to figure out the principle of the beam, so that, whatever weight we put on one side, they could balance it with weights on the other. In *How Children Fail* I described some of the work that very bright fifth-graders did with this beam. One girl, that I can remember, seemed to know how to do at least the simple balancing problems – two weights on one side balancing one on the other. Hardly anyone else in the class could consistently work out even simple problems; most of them never got beyond the guessing stage. And this in spite of the fact that we – or so we thought – had done everything possible to set up a situation that would make discovery more easy. We worked with the children in small groups; we gave each child an easy problem; we encouraged the other children in the group to say whether they thought his solution to the problem was correct, and if not, why not. We thought we had set up in our class a laboratory in miniature, and that the children would accordingly act like scientists. But we hadn't, and they didn't, for just this reason, that it was our problem they were working on, not theirs.

Two years later, when I was teaching my own fifth grade, I borrowed some extra balance beams from Bill, to see whether my students could make anything of them. I put these beams, and some weights to hang on them, on a table at one end of my classroom. Then I had a piece of undeserved good luck. Before I had a chance to do any talking or explaining or instructing about these beams, some children came in early one morning and saw them. 'What's that stuff?' they said. I said, 'Oh, some junk I got from Bill Hull.' They said, 'What's it for?' I said, 'Nothing special; mess around with it if you want to.' Three or four of them went down to the end table and began to fool around. As other children arrived they went down to watch. By half-an-hour later, almost all the kids who had been working with the beams, knew how to work them – including some who were not good students. I gave one of them one of the problems that had in earlier years given very able students so much trouble. She solved it easily and showed that she knew what she was doing. I said, 'You have any trouble figuring that out?' She said, 'Oh no, it was cinchy.'

Not long after, Bill Hull and some other friends of mine were developing a very ingenious and powerful set of mathematical and logical materials (now produced by the McGraw-Hill Book Company in St Louis, Mo.) called Attribute Blocks or A-blocks. These are a set of wooden blocks, of various colours, sizes, and shapes, with which children can play a wide variety of classifying games, and with which they do a great many things that experts on such matters have said they would be unable to do.

They developed these materials by having small groups of young children, mostly five-year-olds, come into their office-lab-classroom and work with them, that is, play various games, do puzzles, solve problems. (Some of the games now incorporated into the unit were invented by the children.) They found a very interesting thing about the way children reacted to these materials. If, when a child came in for the first time, they tried to get him 'to work' right away, to play some of their games and solve some of their puzzles, they got nowhere. The child would try to do what he was asked to do, but without joy or insight. But if at first they let the child alone for a while, let him play with the materials in his own way, they got very different results. At first, the children would work the pieces of wood into a fantasy. Some pieces would be mommies and daddies, some children; or they would be houses and cars; or big animals and little animals. Then the children would make various kinds of patterns, buildings, and constructions out of the pieces of wood. When, through such play and fantasy, the children had taken these materials into their minds, mentally swallowed and digested them, so to speak, they were then ready and willing to play very complicated games, that in the more organized and businesslike situation had left other children completely baffled. This proved to be so consistently true that the experimenters made it a rule always to let children have a period of completely free play with the materials, before asking them to do directed work with them.

David Hawkins, Professor of Philosophy at the University of Colorado and formerly Director of the Elementary Science Study, has written perceptively and eloquently on this question, in an article called 'Messing About in Science', which appeared in the February 1965 issue of *Science and Children*, and also in the June 1966 quarterly report of Educational Services, Inc. He says in part:

(in science teaching, and other aspects of elementary education) there is a time, much greater in amount than commonly allowed, which should be devoted to free and unguided exploratory work (call it play if you wish; I call it work). Children are given materials and equipment – *things* – and are allowed to construct, test, probe, and experiment without superimposed questions or instruction. I call this phase 'Messing About'. . . . In some jargon, this kind of situation is called 'unstructured', which is misleading; some doubters call it chaotic, which it need never be. 'Unstructured' is misleading because there is always a kind of structure to *what* is presented in a class . . .

Let me cite an example from my own recent experiences. Simple frames, each designed to support two or three weights on strings, were handed out one morning in a fifth-grade class. There was one such frame for each pair of children. In two earlier trial classes, we had introduced the same equipment with a much more 'structured' beginning, demonstrating the striking phenomenon of coupled pendula and raising questions about it before the laboratory work was allowed to begin. If there was guidance this time, however, it came only from the apparatus – a pendulum is to swing!

In the front hall of the Urban School, an evening summer school in Boston where I teach English, we have one of these pendulum frames. Some students (high-school age), as they come in, fool around with the pendula. Others do not. One boy came in the other night, looked suspiciously at the pendulum for a while, and then said, 'What's it supposed to be doing?' Children who have spent much time in school no longer surprise me with such questions. I said, 'It's not *supposed* to be doing anything. Shall we tell it to do something?' He didn't get the point of the

joke, or even know that I was joking. Nor did he even so much
as touch the pendulum. It was dangerous. If he didn't know what
it was 'supposed' to do, he wasn't going to try to make it do
anything; it might do the wrong thing, and someone might
think it was his fault. It was a small but striking example of the
feeling described in *How Children Fail*, on the part of many
children, that nature and the universe are not only inconsistent
and unpredictable, but even unfriendly and treacherous.

I started messing with the pendula myself. I knew, not as a
a rule I had memorized, but as part of my mental model of how
the world works, that short pendula swing back and forth more
rapidly than long ones. I had forgotten the exact relationship
between length and rate of swing. My faint hunch was that if
one pendulum was half as long as the other, it would make
two swings for the other's one. I tried this out, found I was
wrong, adjusted the short pendulum until it was making two
swings for one of the other, and estimated by eye that its string
was one quarter as long. From this I re-created the rule. As I
was busy with this little project, one of the other teachers, a very
lively and intelligent woman, began to watch me. After hardly
more than a few seconds she began to say, with some real
anxiety in her voice, 'What rule is it supposed to be following?
What's the rule that applies to what it's doing?' I laughed, and
said, 'Why don't you just watch it for a while, and see what you
see?' But she could not, or would not, play this childlike game.
After some more rather nervous talk about the rule, and how
she never had been able to remember those rules, and never had
been any good at science – all good standard defensive strategies
– she went off about her business.

To return to Professor Hawkins:

In starting this way I, for one, naïvely assumed that a couple of
hours of 'Messing About' would suffice. After two hours, instead, we
allowed two more and, in the end, a stretch of several weeks. In all
this time, there was little or no evidence of boredom or confusion.
Most of the questions we might have planned for came up un-
scheduled.

Why did we permit this length of time? First, because in our previous classes we had noticed that things went well when we veered towards 'Messing About' and not as well when we held too tight a rein on what we wanted the children to do. It was clear that these children had had insufficient acquaintance with the sheer phenomenon of pendulum motion and needed to build an apperceptive background, against which a more analytical sort of knowledge could take form and make sense.

In other words, to use my own way of putting this, until their mental models of the world had enough pendula in them so that talk about pendula would mean something to them. This applies just as strongly to reading, or numbers, or arithmetic, or history, or geography, or language, as it does to science. Children need what we rarely give them in school – time for 'Messing About' with reading – before they start trying to learn to read, to make the connexions between letters and sounds. They need time to build up in their minds, without hurry, without pressure, a sense of what words look like, before they start trying to memorize particular words. In the same way, they need time for 'Messing About' with numbers and numerals, before they start – if they ever should start – trying to memorize addition facts and multiplication tables. They need to know how big 76 is, or 134, or 35,000, or a million. They need to see, again without hurry or pressure, how numbers change and grow and relate to each other. They need to build up a mental model of the territory before they start trying to talk about it. We teachers like to think that we can transplant our own mental models into the minds of children by means of explanations. It can't be done.

Professor Hawkins continues:

Second, we allowed things to develop this way because we decided we were getting a new kind of feedback from the children and were eager to see where and by what paths their interests would evolve and carry them. We were rewarded with a higher level of involvement and a much greater diversity of experiments. Our role was only to move from spot to spot, being helpful but never consciously prompting or directing. In spite of – because of! – this lack of direction, these fifth-graders became very familiar with pendula. They varied the conditions of motion in many ways. . . . There were many sorts of discoveries made, but we let them slip by without much adult resonance, beyond our spontaneous and manifest enjoyment of the phenomena. So discoveries were made, noted, lost, and made again. I think this is why the slightly pontifical phrase 'discovery method' bothers me. When learning is at the most fundamental level, as it is here, with all the abstractions of Newtonian mechanics just around the corner, don't rush! When the mind is evolving the abstractions which will lead to physical comprehension, all of us must cross the line between ignorance and insight many times before we truly understand.

This is exactly the process I am trying to describe in the chapter on reading, where I tell about the five-year-old teaching herself to read. 'When the mind is evolving the abstractions. . . .' In practice, this means that you get a faint hunch, lose it, get it again, test it, lose it again, get it again – and all this many times over. You think that a word says such and such; it seems to work; you meet the word again, and try a new hunch; it doesn't work, causes an inconsistency; you correct the mistake, and go on. After many times, you know the word. You have not memorized it; you know it. It is part of your model of the way things are; you could no more 'forget' it than you could forget that if you drop your shoe, it will fall to the floor, not rise to the ceiling.

One other point. Professor Hawkins rightly says, 'All of us must cross the line between ignorance and insight many times before we truly understand.' Not only must we cross that line many times, but, in the words of the old spiritual, nobody else can cross it for us, we must cross it by ourselves. Being shoved or dragged across does no good.

Professor Hawkins again:

This [Messing About] phase is important, above all, because it carries over into school that which is the source of most of what children have already learned, the roots of their moral, intellectual, and aesthetic development. If education were defined, for the moment, to include everything that children have learned since birth, everything that has come to them from living in the natural and the human world, then by any sensible measure what has come before age five or six would outweigh all the rest. When we narrow the scope of education to what goes on in schools, we throw out the method of that early and spectacular progress at our peril. ... To continue the cultivation of earlier ways of learning, therefore; to find *in school* the good beginnings, the liberating involvements that will make the kindergarten seem a garden to the child and not a dry and frightening desert, this is a need that requires much emphasis on the style of work I have called 'Messing About'. Nor does the garden in this sense end with a child's first school year, or his tenth, as though one could then put away childish things. As time goes on, through a good mixture of this with other phases of work, 'Messing About' evolves with the child and thus changes its quality. It becomes a way of working that is no longer childish, though it remains always childlike, the kind of self-disciplined probing and exploring that is the essence of creativity ...

If you once let children evolve their own learning along paths of their choosing, you then must see it through and *maintain* the individuality of their work. You cannot begin that way and then say, in effect, 'That was only a teaser,' thus using your adult authority to devalue what the children themselves, in the meantime, have found most valuable. So if 'Messing About' is to be followed by, or evolve into, a stage where work is more externally guided and disciplined, there must be at hand what I call 'Multiply Programmed' material; material that contains written and pictorial guidance of some sort for the student, but which is designed for the greatest possible variety of topics, ordering of topics, etc., so that for almost any given way into a subject that a child may evolve on his own, there is material available which he will recognize as helping him farther along that very way. Heroic teachers have sometimes done this on their own, but it is obviously one of the places where designers of curriculum materials can be of enormous help, designing those materials with a rich variety of choices for teacher and child, and freeing the teacher from the role of 'leader-dragger' along a single preconceived path, giving the teacher encouragement and real logistical help in diversifying the activities of a group.

We must recognize that there are some teachers who like being 'leader-draggers'. They like to feel that they are at every moment in control, not only of the child's body, but also of his mind. They like to feel themselves the source and the sole source of all knowledge, wisdom, and learning in the classroom. Some such teachers are moved by a love of power, of which the class-room gives them plenty; others, by a deep and sometimes desperate need to feel useful, necessary, and even indispensable to their students. Both kinds are strongly threatened by any suggestion that children can and should learn on their own. Many other teachers would like to give their students more independence and self-direction, but are held back by a fear of the standardized tests by which their pupils, and they them-selves, will be judged. In any school whose main business is pre-paring children to get high scores on achievement tests, regents' exams, merit scholarship exams, college boards, and the like, we are not likely to see much open-ended, independent student work. It must be said in fairness, too, that so far not many of the curriculum reformers and educational revolutionaries have shown much interest in it either. They tend to be so sure that the path they have marked out for their students is the best of all possible paths, that their main concern is how to lead or drag them down it as fast as possible.

Professor Hawkins again:

There is a common opinion, floating about, that a rich diversity of classroom work is possible only when a teacher has small classes. 'Maybe *you* can do that, but you ought to try it in my class of forty-three!' I want to be the last person to belittle the importance of small classes. But in this particular case, the statement ought to be made that in a large class one cannot afford *not* to diversify chil-dren's work – or rather *not* to allow children to diversify, as they inevitably will, if given the chance. So-called 'ability grouping' is a popular answer today, but it is no answer at all to the real ques-tions of motivation. Groups which are lumped as equivalent with respect to the usual measures are just as diverse in their tastes and spontaneous interests as unstratified groups. ... When children have no autonomy in learning everyone is likely to be bored.

The question of small classes is one I hear every time I speak. My answer is that in a small class you may be able to maintain at least the illusion that you have complete control, and that everyone is doing the same thing at the same time; in a large class it becomes impossible. Given fairly docile children, in classes of about 20, a teacher has a chance of being a reasonably effective policeman. In a class of 40, it can't be done. There are too many to watch. The large classes which exist in many of our schools, and which are, if anything, going to get bigger rather than smaller, require that we find ways to break the academic lockstep, and get our students learning on their own. This is above all essential in our cities, where many children, unlike children in the suburbs, cannot and will not submit to being bored all day long. Many people talk as if our problem was to make city schools as good as the ones in the suburbs. This is not the problem at all. We have been able to afford boredom and mis-education in the suburbs because the children have been willing to put up with it – though we may not be able to afford it there much longer. We can't afford it in the city, because the children won't put up with it, and we have no way to make them. Nothing less than real education will solve the problems of our city schools – and real education means the kind of learning Professor Hawkins is talking about.

Some social-studies teachers asked me once, at a meeting, how students might explore and learn independently in their field. For part of an answer, I told a few stories. The first is about a seven-year-old boy. One day he saw, and read, I think in the *National Geographic*, an article about underwater swimming. Like most kids, he was very interested in the scuba equipment, and even more in the varied and colourful fish the divers were seeing and catching, in the whole idea of an underwater world with a life of its own. Excited, he talked to his mother about the article. Soon after, she found him another article about divers. This time, however, they were not diving for fish, but for treasure – vases, bowls, implements, and weapons, lying deep in the hold of a ship that three thousand years before had sunk in the Mediterranean. Everything about this story fascinated the boy, above all the idea that these strange and beautiful objects had been lying there, unknown, forgotten, for so long. He became interested in the Pre-Homeric civilizations of Crete and Mycenae that had made these treasures. Helpful adults found him some books about them, which he read. In them mention was made of Homer, and the Trojan War, so he read some abridged versions of the *Iliad* and the *Odyssey*. Somewhere in his reading about Troy, he read about the seven cities of Troy, and about Schliemann, the archaeologist who dug them up. He was fascinated with the idea that a city might simply disappear under the ground, and another city be built right on top of it, and so seven times over; he was equally fascinated with the idea of patiently bringing those buried cities into the light again. This made him want to find out as much as he could about archaeology. When I last heard of him, he was reading everything on that subject that he could get his hands on.

The next stories are about a one-room country school taught by Julia Weber (now Gordon). She wrote about her work in a book called *My Country School Diary*, now out of print, though its publishers, Harper's, may bring it out in paperback. The children in the school were in grades 1–8. Much of the time, of necessity, they worked independently. At other times they discussed things, as a class. In these discussions, many questions were raised, and it was Miss Weber's custom to write down many of the unanswered questions on large sheets of paper and post them on the wall, where the children could see them and be reminded of them. The students did not have to find answers to these questions; they were not curriculum, or homework. But they were free to pursue any that particularly interested them. Some questions were never answered. Others caught the curiosity of the class, and led them on some wide-ranging explorations.

One such question came up early one spring, when the children were getting ready to put away their winter clothes. The clothes had to be cleaned before they were put away, and someone asked why they couldn't be washed. Many of them knew that it was because the wool would shrink. But why did wool shrink, and what happened when it shrank? Nobody knew. Perhaps they could find out if they looked at wool through a microscope. Unfortunately, they didn't have a microscope, and couldn't possibly afford to buy one. All right, they would borrow one. They wrote a letter – I believe it was to the State University – asking if they could borrow a microscope and explaining what they wanted to use it for. Incidentally, the children always wrote such letters, and they were writing them all the time, since their tiny school had to borrow most of the books and equipment they needed.

Here, it seems to me, is the answer to the current superstition, made fashionable by Dr Conant and others, that we have to have giant school-factories, because we can't get good education in a school unless it has all the latest equipment. In making our schools ever larger we have lost much more of value than we have gained, and what little we have gained by having all this expensive material in each school, we might well have accomplished in other ways. There could have been, as in some parts of the country there still are, central libraries from which books or equipment could be borrowed, or mobile libraries and laboratories that visit schools in turn. Someday, if we get over our notion that bigness in education means efficiency and quality, we may revive some of those ideas.

At any rate, the microscope eventually arrived – the children had had many other things to work on while they were waiting for it. There was much excitement while they carefully unpacked it, and read the instructions for using it, and learned to use it. Soon they were ready to examine some wool fibres before and after washing. They discovered that the fibres of wool have joints, rather like a telescope, and that for some reason these slide in together when the wool is washed. Then, having looked at wool, they decided to look at a number of other fabrics under the microscope – linen, cotton, rayon. They noticed the different appearances of the fibres themselves, and also, that the appearance of the cloth depended on the way it was woven. This in turn got them interested in weaving, and after some discussion they decided they wanted to weave some cloth of their own, using the simplest kind of tools. More letters were written, and after a while they had all they needed to spin and weave cloth, beginning with raw wool. They decided on wool because it was the easiest to work, using simple tools. They got raw wool from a neighbour who owned sheep; then they washed it, carded it, spun it, and wove it. Someone in the class thought it would be interesting to find out how much work it would take to make the cloth. They decided to keep records of time spent on the project, and so developed or discovered the idea of the man-hour as a unit of work – a very important concept in economics.

When they had finished weaving their small square of cloth, their records showed that seventy-two man-hours had been spent. Seventy-two hours for this tiny square of cloth! How long would it take to make a whole suit? This brought in a good deal of arithmetic, plus the problem of calculating the area of an odd-shaped object. When they found out how long it would take, at their rate, to make a suit, they began to wonder how people like the early colonists ever managed to find time to make their own clothes. They also began to see how great and real was the need for specializing labour, and for labour-saving devices.

The cloth project led the children in a number of different directions. For one thing, they wanted to dye the cloth, so they had to find out about natural dyes, how they were made and used. Since most of these came from plants, this led into botany. They made some dyes, and tested them. They also got interested in other kinds of wool fabric. Their piece of homespun did not look much like the wool garments they were used to seeing and wearing. What caused the difference? How many different kinds of wool were there? The children took to asking everyone they saw wearing wool, what kind of wool they were wearing. They found out that there were many kinds of wool. Someone began to note, on a map, the kinds of animals that gave wool, and the parts of the world they lived in. This led them to wonder, and to discuss, why some kinds of wool cost more than others. After talking and reading about it, they decided that it had to do with the animal, how hard he was to raise and keep, how much wool he gave, and also with the difficulty of making the wool into cloth, how far it had to be shipped, and so on. More genuine economics, and some geography on the side.

At the same time they became interested in the difference between woollens and worsteds (which I don't know), and the weaving process and industry. They could see how better machines would reduce the price of cloth. Who invented the first machines? To get answers to such questions, they had to order books from the county library. Dr Gordon told me that in a year the class of 35 children borrowed 700 books. They found many of the early machines were invented in England. Why there? Partly because there was already a certain amount of division of labour, so that they were in effect ready for the factory mode of organization. What were factories like? They visited a textile mill in New Jersey, read about the early factories and the conditions of labour, talked about the effect of machines on employment, examined the effect of machines on a nearby township, considered labour unions and labour legislation. And so on.

Now, not all the children did all of these things. On the other hand, these were not the only things that the children did. While they were exploring these questions, they were exploring many others as well. And while it was true that only a few of the children might do the actual research on the invention of the first weaving machines, they would always report to the entire class what they had found out, so that almost all the discoveries made were shared by all the children.

Here is another of their projects. The older children used to put out a small school newspaper which appeared every few weeks. One day a student said, 'If it takes us so long to put out this little paper, how come people are able to put out a great, fat newspaper every day?' The question was interesting to the class, as it has always been to me. They decided to look into the matter. After some letters, they were able to visit a large newspaper plant. They were so interested in the type-setting and printing processes that they began to investigate the whole history of type, printing, and book-making. This made some of them curious about the history of writing and writing materials in general. They began to study the earliest alphabets, and such writing materials as papyrus, parchment, and so on. Before long they decided to make – write, type, and bind – a book of their own, about the complete history of writing, printing, and book-making. It was a big job; they had not quite finished by the end of the school year, and a number of them came to school for a week or more after school ended, so that they could finish. Dr Gordon showed me their book. It was a wonderful piece of work: well organized, clearly written, elegantly illustrated and typed, and strongly bound – a real book. In making it, they had gone from today's daily paper all the way back to the beginnings of history.

These stories show us a number of things about the ways in which children learn. They see the world as a whole, mysterious perhaps, but a whole none the less. They do not divide it up into airtight little categories, as we adults tend to do. It is natural for them to jump from one thing to another, and to make the kinds of connexions that are rarely made in formal classes and textbooks. They make their own paths into the unknown, paths that we would never think of making for them. Thus, for example, if we decided that it was important for children to know about the Trojan War, or archaeology, would we start by talking to them about scuba divers? Certainly not. Even if we did, there are many children for whom this would not be a good beginning, or a beginning at all. Finally, when they are following their own noses, learning what they are curious about, children go faster, cover more territory than we would ever think of trying to mark out for them, or make them cover.

People have often said to me, nervously or angrily, that if we let children learn what they want to know they will become narrow specialists, nutty experts in baseball batting averages and such trivia. Not so. Many adults do this; the universities are full of people who have shut themselves up in little fortresses of artificially restricted private learning. But healthy children, still curious and unafraid, do not learn this way. Their learning does not box them in; it leads them out into life in many directions. Each new thing they learn makes them aware of other new things to be learned. Their curiosity grows by what it feeds on. Our task is to keep it well supplied with food.

The Mind at Work

One of the puzzles we had in my fifth-grade class was a geometrical puzzle called *Hako*. You began with a number of thin, flat, rectangular plastic pieces arranged a certain way in a shallow box. The aim was to slide them around, without turning them or lifting them out of the box, so as to finish with the largest piece, a square, at the opposite end of the box from which it started. Though I spent many hours on it, I was never able to do it. This exasperated me. What exasperated me even more was that I seemed to be able to prove that the puzzle was impossible – though I knew it was not. Like most people, I began by moving the pieces around in a kind of blind, haphazard way. Before long, and unwisely, I grew impatient with this. There were too many possible moves, this could go on for ever. The thing to do was use the brain and figure it out. So, moving the pieces very carefully, and analysing each move, I deduced that in order to get the large piece from the top to the bottom, certain other things had to happen along the way. There had to be a point at which certain of the pieces were going up past the big piece while it was going down. Then, still carefully analysing, I showed that this could only happen if certain other pieces moved in certain ways. Finally, I proved that they could not be moved in those ways. Therefore the problem was impossible.

The trouble was, I knew it wasn't impossible. Companies don't sell impossible puzzles; they would be sued, or worse. Besides, the puzzle had been mentioned in the *Scientific American*. Besides that, and worst of all, some students had done it. With all my heart I wanted to believe that they had lied or cheated, but I couldn't convince myself; they weren't the type.

I remember thinking furiously, 'I suppose anyone could do this puzzle if he were willing to sit in front of it like a nitwit, moving the pieces around blindly, until just by dumb luck he happened to get it. I haven't got time for that sort of thing.' More to the point, I felt above that sort of thing.

I went back to the puzzle many times, hoping that I would find some fresh approach to it; but my mind kept moving back into the little groove it had made for itself. I tried to make myself forget my supposed proof that the problem was impossible. No use. Before long I would be back at the business of trying to find the flaw in my reasoning. I never found it. Like many other people, in many other situations, I had reasoned myself into a box. Looking back at the problem, and with the words of Professor Hawkins in my ears, I saw my great mistake. I had begun to reason too soon, before I had allowed myself enough 'Messing About', before I had built a good enough mental model of the ways in which those pieces moved, before I had given myself enough time to explore all the possible ways in which they could move. The reason some of the children were able to do the puzzle was not that they did it blindly, but that they did not try to solve it by reason until they had found by experience what the pieces could do. Because their mental model of the puzzle was complete, it served them; because mine was incomplete, it failed me.

In one of the classes I previously shared with Bill Hull, we worked a good deal with a three-dimensional puzzle named *Soma*, also described and discussed in the *Scientific American*. In this, twenty-seven cubes of wood were glued together to make six four-cube pieces and one three-cube piece. The aim was to use these seven pieces to make various other shapes, beginning with a cube and other simple shapes, and going on to more complicated and difficult shapes such as the Tunnel, the Bath-tub, the Castle, etc. It was a splendid puzzle, one of the very best I have ever seen, among other reasons because children can work on it at many different degrees of difficulty.

My first meeting with this puzzle was embarrassing. A person familiar with it can make the cube in less than half-a-minute in any one of several different ways. By the time I started trying to make the cube, a number of the children were able to do it in about fifteen seconds. My first effort took me about fifty minutes. I tried to keep my struggles out of the sight of the children, but there were some pointed questions. Fortunately I was able to avoid falling into the trap of analysing too soon, perhaps only because I could not see how to. Unable to think of any 'sensible' way to proceed, I fiddled with the pieces, trying to fit them this way and that, making mistakes, working myself into dead ends, going back and starting again. One of the frustrating things about this particular puzzle is that if you have it almost right, you know you have it entirely wrong. When you find yourself saying, 'If this piece just looked like that piece, I could do it,' you have to start almost from the beginning. By many such trials and errors, retrials and corrections, I was finally able, like many of the children, to build up a good mental model of the way these pieces worked. With this model I could tell, without having to try it out, that a certain piece, or even combination of pieces, would not go in a certain spot, and could see several pieces in advance when I was going wrong. Before long I became one of the class experts.

Such experiences suggest a reason why so much that seems to me trivial, misleading, or downright false, has been written about child psychology. The psychologists, on the whole, have not done enough of Professor Hawkins's 'Messing About'. They have not seen enough children in their native habitat – homes, schools, playgrounds, streets, stores, anywhere. They haven't talked or played with enough of them, or helped them, or comforted them, or coerced them, or made them pleased, or excited, or rebellious, or angry. Unless he is very fortunate, a young psychologist is very likely to have his head stuffed full of theories of children before he has had a chance to look at any. When he does start looking at them, it is likely to be in very special laboratory or testing situations. Like many teachers, he may not recognize the many ways in which children betray anxiety, because he has never seen them in a situation in which they were not anxious. Also, like me trying to do the puzzle, he may be so much a prisoner of his theories that he cannot see anything that does not fit into them.

For such reasons I would like to stress again what I said very early in this book. My aim in writing it is not primarily to persuade educators and psychologists to swap new doctrines for old, but to persuade them to *look* at children, patiently, repeatedly, respectfully, and to hold off making theories and judgements about them until they have in their minds what most of them do not now have – a reasonably accurate model of what children are like.

I should add, too, that I am not trying to deny the importance of close, deductive, analytical, logical reasoning. In its proper place, it is a useful, powerful, often essential tool. I am only trying to say that out of its place, it is likely to be not only useless but harmful, and that its place is not everywhere. It works when we have a very limited amount of evidence, all we are going to get, and from it have to reconstruct the past – find out who committed a crime, or how and why an accident took place, or what is ailing in a particular man, or machine. It works when we can limit and isolate, one by one, the variables we have to deal with. Thus the skilled repair-man, trying to find out why a machine is working badly, checks its various elements, one by one, until he finds the one that is causing the trouble. Thus the scientist, meeting a new phenomenon in the lab, changes, one by one, the conditions of the experiment until he finds the one that seems to affect the phenomenon. And we use this kind of reasoning to check our hypotheses, our theories or hunches about why things work as they do. We say, 'If this theory is true, then certain other things ought to happen,' and then we find out whether in fact they do happen. If they do, the theory is confirmed, temporarily, at least. The story is told of Einstein that, after the observations of some astronomers seemed to have confirmed his Theory of Relativity, a woman congratulated him on his theory having been proved right. He said, 'Madam, a thousand experiments can never prove me right; a single experiment can prove me wrong.' Even when the facts seem to support our reasoning, we must, like Einstein, not assume that we have found the final truth.

But if there are times and places and conditions where this kind of reasoning is useful, there are others where it does not work at all. If the experience before us is completely new and strange; if there is much new material to be observed, material that doesn't seem to fall into any recognizable pattern order; if we cannot tell what are the variables that influence the situation, much less isolate them, we will be unwise to try to think like a detective, or a scientist in a laboratory.

Some years ago, some sociologists were trying to draw analogies between the behaviour of molecules in a gas and the behaviour of human beings in society, and from there between the laws that describe or explain the behaviour of gases and comparable laws that would supposedly describe and explain the behaviour of human beings in society. This is a very good example of how not to use the scientific method. In such situations, we must use our minds very differently. We must clear them of preconceived notions, we must suspend judgement, we must open ourselves to the situation, take in as much data as we can, and wait patiently for some kind of order to appear out of the chaos. In short, we must think like a little child.

It may be useful to describe a few situations in which I had to, and was able to, make myself think this way. One bright summer day some friends took me to the Haystack School of Arts and Crafts in Maine. There, for the first time, I saw a hand loom. One of the teachers had it out in the sunshine, on one of the many broad, wooden terraces that look down a hill and over the sea. She was setting it up for some weaving, and my hosts gathered around to talk about what she was doing and was planning to do.

After looking at the machine a while, and listening to this informed talk, I felt the faint beginnings of anxiety. A hand loom is a very open machine; all the parts of it can be clearly seen. It seemed to me that after some careful looking and reasoning I ought to be able to figure out how this machine worked. But

I couldn't. It looked like nothing but a jumble and confusion of little parts, wires, and scraps of wood. None of it made any sense at all. Nor could I think how to make sense of it. Where to begin?

In such situations we tend to have a defensive reaction, which I began to sense in myself. Confronted with what it cannot grasp, the mind tends to turn away, to shut it out. We say to ourselves, 'Oh, well, who cares about looms and weaving, anyway?' We seek the relief of thinking about something that we can grasp and understand. Having learned to recognize this protective and cowardly strategy, I would not allow myself to use it. I thought, 'Come on, now, quit acting like a scared kid.' I examined the loom more carefully, and began to ask myself intelligent questions. What's this for? Where does this lead? But no use. It remained as much a mystery as ever. The anxiety grew, with a little shame added. Some of this was caused by not being able to make sense of the loom. Some was caused by my feeling that as a supposedly fairly intelligent man I ought to be able to make sense out of it. Like children in school, I was worried by the fear of not being able to live up to my own concept of myself. Finally, I knew that everyone else around me knew how that loom worked, and knew that I didn't. I could almost hear them thinking, 'Funny about John, he's usually pretty smart about most things, yet that simple loom, that you would think anyone could understand, is too much for him.' Then, to make matters worse, they began to try to help by giving explanations. They spoke with that infuriating mixture of indulgence and impatience with which the expert always explains things to the non-expert. It is always gratifying to be able to understand what someone else cannot; and more gratifying yet to make yourself his benefactor, by explaining it to him; and still more gratifying – unless you are required to make him understand – if in spite of your explanation he continues not to understand. In this spirit my friends began to say, 'It's really very simple; this piece here . . .'

After a certain amount of this I said, rather sharply, 'Please stop talking about it, and just let me look at it.' I thought to myself, 'Remember what you have learned about learning. Be like a child. Use your eyes. Gag that teacher's mouth inside your head, asking all those questions. Don't try to analyse this thing, look at it, take it in.' And shutting out of mind the knowing conversation of the others, I did so. Now and then the voice inside would begin to ask questions. I silenced it, and for some time went on looking.

There were many other things to see: potters, print makers, and most exciting of all, glass blowers. After seeing them all, we started home. And as we drove a most extraordinary thing began to happen. I was not thinking about the loom; as my host was a potter, we were talking mostly about the pottery. But as we talked, a loom began slowly to put itself together in my mind. There is no other way to describe it. Suddenly, for no reason, the image of a particular part would suddenly appear in my consciousness, but in such a way that I understood what that part was for. When I say 'understood', I don't mean that some kind of verbal explanation went along with it. I mean that I could see what the part was for and what it did, I could almost see it doing its work. If I had been building a loom and had had that part in my hand, I would have known where to put it.

This loom-building process was very slow. It would be interesting to have a record of the order in which the parts of this loom appeared and assembled themselves, but I have none. Sensing that something important was happening in the non-verbal, non-conscious part of my mind, I did not want to look too hard at the process, lest I bring it to a stop. Also, I had no way of knowing, at any time, how much farther it would go. When the first part of the loom appeared in my surprised consciousness, I had no reason to believe that other parts would later appear in the same way. However, they did, some during our trip home, others during the rest of the day, some even the following day. By the end of that day, a loom had made itself in my mind. There was a working model of a loom in there. If I had to build a loom, I would have known at least roughly what parts were needed and where they went. There was much about the loom that I didn't know, but I now knew where knowledge left off and ignorance began; knew the questions I needed to ask; knew enough to be able to make sense of the answers. Some of what people had told me, trying to explain the loom, came back to me, and now I could see what their words meant.

Explanations. We teachers – perhaps all human beings – are in the grip of an astonishing delusion. We think that we can take a picture, a structure, a working model of something, constructed in our minds out of long experience and familiarity, and by turning that model into a string of words, transplant it whole into the mind of someone else. Perhaps once in a thousand times, when the explanation is extraordinary good, and the listener extraordinarily experienced and skilful at turning word-strings into non-verbal reality, and when explainer and listener share in common many of the experiences being talked about, the process may work, and some real meaning may be communicated. Most of the time, explaining does not increase understanding, and may even lessen it.

A few years ago I spent an evening, at Bill Hull's house, in the company of a number of people who were all interested in teaching mathematics to children. For most of the evening we talked about things we had done in classes, or were thinking of doing. As the party began to break up, one of the group, a most distinguished visitor from abroad, confessed that although most of the materials he had developed for children dealt with numbers and numerals, or with algebra, his own real love was geometry. Not the old-fashioned plane geometry that most people have met in school, but a much more advanced and exotic geometry. Memory tells me that he called it projective geometry, though it didn't sound like the only projective geometry I had ever read about. I asked him what he liked so much about this branch of mathematics. He replied that it was the beauty and simplicity of the theorems. 'Such as what?' I asked. It was a mistake. His eyes flashed with enthusiasm. Such as the proof that the intersection of two quartics is a twisted cubic. Seeing a glazed look in my eyes, he began to sketch the proof. I held up a hand, laughing, and said, 'Whoa, wait a minute, I've never even heard of these things, I don't know what a quartic or a cubic is, much less a twisted cubic.' Too late. The teaching fit was on him. He began to 'explain'. As he saw that I still did not understand, he began to grow exasperated – like most teachers when their 'explanations' are not being understood. 'It's really very simple!' he said, as his hands sketched complicated shapes in the air. I was amused, but appalled. Here was a really great teacher, who for years had been working with young children trying to find ways to have them experience and discover, with hands and eyes, the relationships of mathematics. Yet in spite of his long experience, he believed so strongly in the magic power of explanations that he thought he could drop me into the middle of an advanced and complex branch of mathematics, in which I had absolutely no knowledge or experience, and with a few words and waves of the hand make the whole thing clear.

Jerome Bruner has said that one thing that happens in school is that children are led to believe they don't know or can't do something that they knew, or could do, before they got to school. I have seen this demonstrated many times, but never as vividly as in the following example, quoted from the prospectus of the Green Valley School, in which George von Hilsheimer writes:

One of our art associates once conducted an experiment in her art resources classroom. As the children entered the classroom they found construction paper on the desks. The teacher held up a folded fan – like those you and I have made many times – 'Know what this is?'

'Oh, yes!'

'Can you make one?'

'Yes! Yes!'

Every child quickly made the little fan. The teacher then read from the book the instructions on how to make the fan. She read slowly, with proper emphasis and phrasing. The instructions were well designed to be clear to the fifth grade mind. After reading, the teacher asked the children to make the fans again. Not one child could make a fan. The teacher sat at each desk and tried to get the children to go back to the first way they had made the fan (with the fan still lying on the desk). They could not.

There have been many such experiments in educational psychology. Unfortunately, few teachers and even fewer school systems take such evidence seriously. We do.

Such stories make many defenders of the system angry. They say, 'But human knowledge is stored and transmitted in symbols. We have to teach children to use them.' True enough. But the only way children can learn to get meaning out of symbols, to turn other people's symbols into a kind of reality or a mental model of reality, is by learning first to turn their own reality into symbols. They have to make the journey from reality to symbol many times, before they are ready to go the other way. We must begin with what children see, do, and know, and have them talk and write about such things, before trying to talk to them much about things they don't know. Thus, given children who knew how to make a paper fan, it might not be a bad idea at all to ask them to try to tell someone else how to make one, without using any gestures, as if they were talking over a phone. I used to ask fifth-graders how they would explain over the phone the difference between right and left, to someone who could speak English but did not happen to know those words. Such games are exciting and useful. But when we do what we do most of the time in school – beginning with meaningless symbols and statements, and try to fill them with meaning by way of explanations, we only convince most children either that all symbols are meaningless or that they are too stupid to get meaning from them.

Perhaps the greatest dangers of becoming too bound up with symbols, too symbol-minded, if I may be allowed the phrase, is that we don't know how to give them up, get them out of the way, when they are of no use to us. We become addicts. There are times when words, symbols, only get between us and reality. At such times, we must be ready to let them go, and use our minds in more appropriate ways – more childlike ways.

Such an experience took place not long ago when I was visiting A. S. Neill at Summerhill School in England. The weather was terrible, the public rooms of the school were deserted, the students were all in their rooms, so there was nothing much to see around the school. Neill himself was laid up in his room with a painful attack of sciatica, and was eager for company. So we had a long and very interesting talk. More than once, thinking I had taken enough of his time, I got up to go, but he waved me back in my chair, where I was more than glad to stay.

At about three o'clock his brother-in-law came in, and asked if he could use the TV to watch the England–Scotland rugby match. Neill asked me if I knew anything about rugby. I said I didn't; he said he didn't either. We decided to watch the game. Before it had gone on two minutes, I found myself in the same panicky confusion that had gripped me when I looked at the loom. Rugby is a hard game for a novice to understand. It is like a crazy combination of soccer and football, just enough like either one to be misleading. As I watched, the teacher-voice in my head began to ask, 'Why did he do that? Why did he put the ball there? Why is he running that way?' And so on. But there were no answers.

After a few futile minutes of this, I saw that this was the loom situation again. I didn't know enough about the game to be able to reason about it. No use to ask questions. Neill couldn't answer them. His brother-in-law – a taciturn man – wouldn't. Anyway, I didn't know enough to know what questions to ask. The only thing to do was to turn off the questions and watch – like a child. Take it all in. See everything, worry about nothing. This is what I did. When the voice inside began to yammer, I silenced it. At half-time I seemed to know no more than at the start. Everything that happened on that field surprised me. During the half the announcers, as in every land, talked learnedly about the play during the first half. Not a word they said made any sense. I listened, like a child listening to adult conversation, taking in the words without knowing or caring what they might mean. Soon the second half started, as puzzling as the first. Then, suddenly, about ten minutes into the period, the patterns of the game all fell into place. Like the loom, the game put itself together in my mind. I suddenly found that I knew what the players were doing, what they were trying to do, what they might do next, why the plays the announcer called good were in fact good, why the mistakes he pointed out were in fact mistakes. There was still much I didn't know, details of the game, rules, penalties. But I knew enough to ask about them, and to make some sense out of the answers.

Not long afterwards, I had another chance to think like a child. Going south from London on a train, I found myself in a compartment – a small, closed-in section seating eight passengers – with a Scandinavian couple. They were talking rapidly in their native language, of which I understood nothing. For a while, I paid no attention, looking at England through the train window, and thinking my own thoughts. Then, after a while, it occurred to me that this was an interesting opportunity to listen to language as a baby listens to it. Still looking out the window, I began to pay close attention to what they were saying. It was very much like listening to a complicated piece of modern music. I have discovered, after hearing many concerts and records, that the best way to listen to strange and unfamiliar music, to keep your attention focused sharply on it, is to try to reproduce the music in your mind – instant imitation. In the same way, I was trying to reproduce in my mind, as soon as I heard them, the sounds made by these people as they talked. I didn't get them all, but I got many of them. Also, though I wasn't looking for patterns – there wasn't time for that – I was alert for them, so that when a sound or word came along that I had heard before, it made an extra impression. It was an interesting and absorbing exercise. By the time forty minutes had passed, and I had reached my stop, I had begun to feel, and almost recognize, a few of the sounds and words in their talk. Perhaps this kind of raw listening would be useful for students studying a foreign language. We might have a record, or a tape, of a voice reading a particular passage, first at rapid conversational speed, then more slowly, finally so slowly that each word could be heard separately. From listening to such tapes, students might become sensitive to the relation between

the separate sounds of a language and the sound of the flow of
the whole language.

*

Let me sum up what I have been trying to say about the natural
learning style of young children. The child is curious. He wants
to make sense out of things, find out how things work, gain competence and control over himself and his environment, do what
he can see other people doing. He is open, receptive, and perceptive. He does not shut himself off from the strange, confused,
complicated world around him. He observes it closely and
sharply, tries to take it all in. He is experimental. He does not
merely observe the world around him, but tastes it, touches it,
hefts it, bends it, breaks it. To find out how reality works, he
works on it. He is bold. He is not afraid of making mistakes. And
he is patient. He can tolerate an extraordinary amount of uncertainty, confusion, ignorance, and suspense. He does not have
to have instant meaning in any new situation. He is willing and
able to wait for meaning to come to him – even if it comes very
slowly, which it usually does.

School is not a place that gives much time, or opportunity,
or reward, for this kind of thinking and learning. Can we make
it so? I think we can, and must. In this book I have tried to suggest, very briefly, how we might do it. To discuss this in any
detail would take a book in itself. What is essential is to realize
that children learn independently, not in bunches; that they
learn out of interest and curiosity, not to please or appease the
adults in power; and that they ought to be in control of their
own learning, deciding for themselves what they want to learn
and how they want to learn it. To such ideas, people react in
many ways, but two reactions appear so regularly that they
seem worth discussing.

The first is often expressed like this: 'Aren't you asking children to discover and re-create, all by themselves, the whole
history of the human race?' It would be easy to dismiss the question as silly, except that so many sensible and serious people ask
it. What trips them up is this word 'discover'. They act as if it

meant 'invent', that is, discover for the first time. But this is not what I mean, or any educators mean, when they talk about the importance of letting children discover things for themselves. We do not ask or expect a child to invent the wheel starting from scratch. He doesn't have to. The wheel has been invented. It is out there, in front of him. All I am saying is that a child does not need to be *told* what wheels are and what they are for, in order to know. He can figure it out for himself, in his own way, in his own good time. In the same way, he does not have to invent the electric light bulb, the aeroplane, the internal combustion engine – or law, government, art, or music. They, too, have been invented, and are out there. The whole culture is out there. What I urge is that a child be free to explore and make sense of that culture in his own way. This is as much discovery as I ask of him, a discovery that he is well able to make.

The second reaction is often expressed like this: 'Aren't there certain things that everyone ought to know, and isn't it our job, therefore, to make sure that children know them?' This argument can be attacked on many fronts. With the possible exception of knowing how to read, which in any case is a skill, it cannot be proved that any piece of knowledge is essential for everyone. Useful and convenient, perhaps; essential, no. Moreover, the people who feel that certain knowledge is essential do not agree among themselves on what that knowledge is. The historians would vote for history; the linguists, for language; the mathematicians, for maths; and so on. In the words of Jimmy Durante, 'Everybody wants to get into the act.' Moreover, the knowledge changes, becomes useless, out of date, or downright false. Believers in essential knowledge decreed that when I was in school I should study physics and chemistry. In physics we used a reputable and then up-to-date college text that announced on page 1 that 'matter was not created nor destroyed'. Of my chemistry, I remember only two or three formulas and a concept called 'valence'. I mentioned valence to a chemist the other day and he laughed. When I asked what was so funny, he said, 'Nobody ever talks about valence any more; it's an outmoded concept.' But the rate of discovery being what it is, the likelihood that what children learn today will be out of date in twenty years is much *greater* than it was when I was a student.

My real reason, however, for believing that the learner, young or old, is the best judge of what he should learn next, is very different. I would be against trying to cram knowledge into the heads of children, even if we could agree on what knowledge to cram, and could be sure that it would not go out of date, even if we could be sure that, once crammed in, it would stay in. Even then, I would trust the child to direct his own learning. For it seems to me a fact that, in our struggle to make sense out of life, the things we most need to learn are the things we most want to learn. To put this another way, curiosity is hardly ever idle. What we want to know, we want to know for a reason. The reason is that there is a hole, a gap, an empty space in our understanding of things, our mental model of the world. We feel that gap like a hole in a tooth and want to fill it up. It makes us ask How? When? Why? While the gap is there, we are in tension, in suspense. Listen to the anxiety in a person's voice when he says, 'This doesn't make sense!' When the gap in our understanding is filled, we feel pleasure, satisfaction, relief. Things make sense again – or at any rate, they make more sense than they did.

When we learn this way, for these reasons, we learn both rapidly and permanently. The person who really needs to know something, does not need to be told many times, drilled, tested. Once is enough. The new piece of knowledge fits into the gap ready for it, like a missing piece in a jigsaw puzzle. Once in place, it is held in, it can't fall out. We don't forget the things that make the world a more reasonable or interesting place for us, that make our mental model more complete and accurate. Now, if it were possible for us to look into the minds of children and see what gaps in their mental models most needed filling, a good case could be made for giving them the information needed to fill them. But this is not possible. We cannot find out what children's mental models are like, where they are distorted, where incomplete. We cannot make direct contact with a child's understanding of the world. Why not? First, because to a very

How Children Learn

considerable extent he is unaware of much of his own understanding. Secondly, because he hasn't the skill to put his understanding into words, least of all words that he could be sure
would mean to us what they meant to him. Thirdly, because
we haven't time. Words are not only a clumsy and ambiguous
means of communication, they are extraordinarily slow. To
describe only a very small part of his understanding of the world,
a man will write a book that takes us days to read.

I think of some good friends of mine. We know each other
well, know each other's interests, speak each other's language.
We may spend an entire evening talking, each of us intent on
gaining a better understanding of the other's thought. At the
end of the evening, with luck, we may each have a very slightly
better idea about what the other thinks, on a very particular
subject. On the other hand, very often an evening of talk, however pleasant and interesting, may only lead us to realize how
little we understand the other, how great are the gulfs and
mysteries between us.

The human mind is a mystery. To a very large extent, it will
probably always be so. We will never get very far in education
until we realize this, and give up the delusion that we can know,
measure, and control what goes on in children's minds. To know
one's own mind is difficult enough. I am, to quite a high degree,
an introspective person. For a long time, I have been interested
in my own thoughts, feelings, and motives, eager to know as
much as I could of the truth about myself. After many years, I
think that at most I may know something about a very small
part of what goes on in my own head. How preposterous to
imagine that I can know what goes on in someone else's.

In my mind's ear I can hear the anxious voices of a hundred
teachers asking me, 'How can you tell, how can you be sure
what the children are learning, or even that they are learning
anything?' The answer is simple. We can't tell. We can't be sure.
What I am trying to say about education rests on a belief that,
though there is much evidence to support it, I cannot prove, and
that may never be proved. Call it a faith. This faith is that man
is by nature a learning animal. Birds fly, fish swim; man thinks

and learns. Therefore, we do not need to 'motivate' children into learning, by wheedling, bribing, or bullying. We do not need to keep picking away at their minds to make sure they are learning. What we need to do, and all we need to do, is bring as much of the world as we can into the school and the classroom; give children as much help and guidance as they need and ask for; listen respectfully when they feel like talking; and then get out of the way. We can trust them to do the rest.

More about Penguins and Pelicans

Penguinews, which appears every month, contains details of all the new books issued by Penguins as they are published. From time to time it is supplemented by *Penguins in Print*, which is a complete list of all books published by Penguins which are in print. (There are well over three thousand of these.)

A specimen copy of *Penguinews* will be sent to you free on request, and you can become a subscriber for the price of the postage. For a year's issues (including the complete lists) please send 4s. if you live in the United Kingdom, or 8s. if you live elsewhere. Just write to Dept EP, Penguin Books Ltd, Harmondsworth, Middlesex, enclosing a cheque or postal order, and your name will be added to the mailing list.

Another Pelican by John Holt
is described on the following page.

Note: *Penguinews* and *Penguins in Print* are not available in the U.S.A. or Canada

Another Pelican by John Holt

How Children Fail

Most children fail to develop more than a small part of their capacity for learning and creating. Afraid, bored, or confused, they fall short; and their failure is sometimes not even noticed.

This book records a teacher's search for the beginnings of an answer to the question why children fail. It developed from the journal which John Holt kept whilst observing children in class. He analyses the strategies children use to meet or dodge the demands which the adult world makes on them, the effect of fear and failure on children, the distinction between real and apparent learning, and the ways in which schools fail to meet the needs of children. His conclusions suggest ways of enriching the experiences of children at school and at home.

'It is possibly the most penetrating, and probably the most eloquent book on education to be published in recent years. To anyone who deals with children and cares about children, it cannot be too highly recommended' — *New York Times*

'John Holt has done a good and necessary job. A very good book indeed' – A. S. Neill

Not for sale in the U.S.A. or Canada